Constitutionalism
in East Africa

Progress, Challenges and Prospects in 1999

Kivutha Kibwana
Chris Maina Peter
Nyangabyaki Bazaara

Fountain Publishers

Fountain Publishers Ltd
P.O. Box 488
Kampala
E-mail: fountain@starcom.co.ug
Website: www.fountainpublishers.com

ISBN 9970 02 286 5

_____

Cataloguing-in-Publication Data

Kivutha Kibwana
Constitutionalism in East Africa: progress, challenges
and prospects in 1999/ Kivutha Kibwana, Chris Maina Peter (and)
Nyangabyaki Bazaara, Kampala: Fountain Publishers, 2002
    p. cm
Includes index
ISBN: 9970-02-286-5

1. Constitutional Development – Kenya
2. Constitution-making – Tanzania
3. Constitutional Development – Uganda. I. Title
342.0'09676–dc 21

Contents

Contributors   ii
Abbreviations   iii
Introduction   v

1. ***Kivutha Kibwana***: Constitutional Development in Kenya   1
   Introduction   1
   The meaning and nature of constitutional development   1
   Constitutional development in historical perspective   3
   Constitutional developments in 1999   5
   NCEC's attempts to break the constitutional impasse   14
   Conclusion: Emerging issues in constitutional
   development in 1999   15

2. ***Chris Maina Peter***: Constitution-making in Tanzania:
   The Role of Civil Society Organisations   18
   Introduction: The constitution and constitution-making   18
   Struggle for independence: The role played by the
   people through civic organisations   19
   Independence and the parting of ways between the
   leaders and the led   20
   Major constitutional changes in the country   21
   The White Paper: The work of the Kisanga Committee   28
   The 13th Amendment of the constitution, April 2000   29
   Conclusion   31

3. ***Nyangabyaki Bazaara***: Mixed Results in Uganda's
   Constitutional Development: An Assessment   40
   Introduction   40
   A violent history of political change and the necessity
   for a new constitution   41
   The Constitutional Commission and the Constituent
   Assembly   45
   Constitutional issues in 1999   47
   Conclusion   59

Contributors

Kivutha Kibwana is Associate Professor of Law at the University of Nairobi.

Chris Maina Peter is Professor of Law at the University of Dar es Salaam.

Nyangabyaki Bazaara is the Executive Director of the Centre for Basic Research, Kampala.

Abbreviations

ADF	Allied Democratic Forces
AIDS	Acquired Immunity Difficiency Syndrome
AIM	African Independence Movement
AMNUT	All Muslim National Union of Tanganyika
ANC	African National Congress
ASP	Afro Shirazi Party
BBC	British Broadcasting Corporation
CA	Constituent Assembly
CCM	Chama Cha Mapinduzi
CGD	Centre for Government and Development
DP	Democratic Party
DPP	Director of Public Prosecutions
ENHAS	Entebbe Handling Service
FAD	Foundation for African Development
IMF	International Monetary Fund
IPPG	Inter Parties Parliamentary Group
JCIPF	Commission of Inquiry into the Police Force
KADU	Kenya African Democratic Union
KANU	Kenya African National Union
KPU	Kenya Peoples Union
KY	Kabaka Yekka
LRA	Lord's Resistance Army
MPs	Members of Parliament
NALU	National Army for the Liberation of Uganda
NCEC	National Executive Council
NCPC	National Convention Planning Committee
NDP	National Development Party
NEP	National Enterprise Party
NGO	Non Governmental Organisation
NRA	National Resistance Army
NRM	National Resistance Movement
NSSF	National Social Security Fund
NUTA	National Union of Tanganyika Workers
PCEA	Presbyterian Church of East Africa
PCP	Peoples Convention Party
PDP	Peoples Democratic Party
RDC	Resident District Commissioner

UDASA	University of Dar es Salaam Academic Staff Assembly
SAPs	Structural Adjustment Programmes
TANU	Tanganyika African National Union
TFL	Tanganyika Federation of Labour
TLS	Tanganyika Law Society
UHRC	Uganda Human Rights Commission
UPC	Uganda Peoples Congress
UPDF	Uganda Peoples Defence Forces
USSR	Union of Soviet Socialist Republics
UTP	United Tanganyika Party

Introduction

From the beginning of the 1990s the winds of democratisation and good governance began to blow over the African continent in the wake of the end of the cold war. Many saw these developments as the second liberation and others, like Thabo Mbeki, the South African president, characterised them as the African renaissance.

Central to the democratisation drive was the process of constitution-making and constitutionalism. The nature and pace of change varied from country to country and from region to region. In some countries like Niger popular insurrections occurred; in much of Francophone Africa the model of the national conference was adopted to hammer out a national consensus and reconstitute the state on a popular democratic basis. In many African countries the edifices of dictatorship seemed to crumble overnight.

Compared to other regions of Africa, there were neither insurrections nor national conferences in East Africa. Instead, a more deliberate and controlled process occurred as exemplified by the work of the constitutional commissions in Tanzania and Uganda.

Although today we may be less sanguine about the extent and depth of change that Africa is undergoing, it is clear that the issue of constitutionalism is alive and manifested in more sharp focus than ever before. Beyond the quest for good governance, the people of East Africa appear to be coming into their own with regard to constitutionalism and are acting less spontaneously. Their pursuit of constitutionalism goes beyond mere constitutional formalities to embrace such aspects as the acceptance, especially by the leaders, to be bound by both the letter and spirit of the constitution; consistent constitutional practices especially with regard to the acquisition and retention of state power, and constitutional change; constitutional stability; as well as the substance of respect of human rights and rule of law – and generally building a constitutional ethic or culture.

When we closely examine these features it becomes clear that it is the leaders that subvert constitutionalism and, therefore, in such circumstances constitutionalism can only be attained by popular participation and vigilance since, in the final analysis, the people are the guarantors of constitutionalism.

This publication reviews constitutional developments in each of the three East African countries (Kenya, Tanzania and Uganda) during the year 1999. Professor Kivutha Kibwana's article on Kenya touches on the purpose and usefulness of such comparative review. The individual country papers were undertaken by experts on constitutionalism in the three countries based on information garnered from diverse sources such as interviews, newspapers, and other publications, court decisions and legislation. In so doing, the country papers examine the progress, challenges and prospects of constitutionalism in East Africa.

These are the first reviews of the state of constitutionalism in the three countries. It is intended that the exercise will be undertaken annually. Each review gives synoptic highlights of the constitutional histories of the three countries, so as to place the constitutional developments of 1999 in a historical context. However, the article on Tanzania differs from those on Kenya and Uganda in the sense that the developments in 1999 do not receive explicit separate treatment but are subsumed under a more general discussion focusing on popular participation in constitution-making.

A comparison of the reviews immediately yields clear commonalities that characterise the state of constitutionalism in East Africa. In the first place, the history of the three countries reveals that governments and ruling parties have made concerted efforts to keep the people at bay in the process of constitution-making. Amongst other things, these histories reveal that governments and ruling parties are averse to popular autonomous participation in constitution-making. Efforts to suppress popular initiatives in this regard are well documented. The attempts to confine any discussion of constitutional matters within the straitjacket of an officially determined agenda, pace and limits are illustrated by the 1983 constitutional debate in Tanzania. There, as Professor Chris Maina Peter points out, the ruling party ordained which areas were to be discussed although, of course, the people did not respect such arbitrary boundaries and the momentum of their debate carried over and gave direction to subsequent significant developments.

Such negative trends reached absurd levels in the case of Uganda's 'pigeon hole' constitution of 1966, where discussion was denied even to the political class itself and parliament was forced to adopt a constitution, copies of which they found in their pigeon holes after the event. This development was perfected by the 1971 military coup, which entailed the unilateral amendment of the constitution by the military junta without recourse to anybody.

The 1999 events in Kenya are a reminder that this problem is very much alive. In that country the convoluted contortions of the ruling party, and those collaborating with it, managed rather successfully to frustrate the process of constitution-making by seeking either to confine it to parliament to the exlusion of civil society or by suppressing it altogether. The histories of the three countries also show that constitutionalism is deliberately undermined by the authorities to avoid comprehensive constitution-making exercises preferring the alternative of the piecemeal, incremental approach which in all three countries has resulted in patchwork constitutions that probably lack coherence as well as the necessary popular support. The exception to this appears to be the protracted constitution-making exercise in Uganda between 1989 and 1993 which Nyangabyaki Bazaara critically discusses in some detail. However, the drawbacks of the constitution-making process, especially its partisan character in Uganda, as well as the contradictions in the resultant constitutional instrument like Article 269 has meant that constitutionalism in that country has been founded on shaky foundations.

Despite the drawbacks to constitutionalism in East Africa, the events in 1999 reveal the resilience of the people in the face of suppression. In this respect, the Kenyan review recounts the activities of a vibrant civil society, especially the considerable role played by the churches and secular sections of organised civil society. Even so, the state has attempted to either infiltrate such organisations or create parallel 'civil society' organisations. The abortive attempt to constitute the Constitution Review Commission in 1999 in Kenya illustrates this very well. It was KANU that flouted the existing law and tried to undermine the efforts of the churches and other organisations. Beyond this particular effort, popular vigilance and a general militant activism by the citizenry have become bulwarks in erecting the edifice of the prerequisites for sustainable constitutionalism. The role of civil society in Tanzania and Uganda, on the other hand, does not resonate with the Kenyan levels. In Tanzania, the active circles revolve around the university and the Law Society; while Uganda's appears to be a far more quiescent civil society with the NGOs setting a conscious and clear dividing line between their perceived mandates, on the one hand, and political action, on the other. This situation can perhaps safely be attributed to the years of fascist military rule and the more militaristic approach to Uganda's politics in general.

In spite of the different levels of animation of civil society in East Africa, it is precisely in the context of its activities that the idea of an annual review of the state of constitutional development lies. Such reviews will not constitute simply a record and its evaluation. To a great extent they will act like mirrors and a resource through which East African civil society–which is the true engine and motive force for durable constitutionalism–will be able to examine itself, compare and co-ordinate levels of organisation and activities, celebrate the milestones on the road to constitutionalism in the three East African countries and press more urgently and coherently reluctant states and ruling parties towards positive change. Fortunately, it is also evident from the reviews that the states and ruling parties are beginning, however reluctantly, to recognise the inevitability of change.

As it is, the developments in 1999 are instructive and offer both positive and negative lessons for the various countries, especially when the country experiences are laid side by side. The opportunity to borrow and exchange ideas and practices is enormous. In this way we can move together and for ever put behind us, to use a phrase in one of the reviews, the 'years of demobilisation of civil society.' And one hopes that in the end these experiences will spill beyond the horizons of East Africa to spread their liberating spirit to a continent whose stunted constitutionalism has caused untold misery to the African people.

How did the three countries compare in terms of the opportunities and constraints as well as the prospects and challenges for constitutionalism in 1999? Kenya's constitutional path faced the hurdles of a recalcitrant state seeking to reverse the gains in the 1998 law on constitutional review which had been based on popular national consensus. The state and the ruling party sought to have a compromised parliament undertake the exercise. Through sabotage, manipulation and stonewalling the state managed to create an impasse in the constitution making process. Also on the negative side was state violence and repression, especially in the face of popular activism; and plain illegality, notably the refusal to appoint a vice president in defiance of the constitution.

On the positive side were the general popular activities to advance the cause of constitutionalism. Such activities involved rallies, protests, demonstrations, riots and public interest litigation. These activities were undertaken by a wide spectrum of society including traders, women, university students, transporters, churches and other organisations.

More specifically, the activities of a direct constitutional nature by the churches and by the National Convention Executive Council kept stoking the fire, keeping alive the prospects of a people-driven constitution review.

In the case of Uganda in 1999, serious cracks showed up in the operationalisation of the 1995 constitution. A good example was the failure to enact various laws such as the political parties law as required by the constitution. The continued civil war, and the involvement of Uganda in the Congo without recourse to parliament were also negative constitutional developments. On the other hand, the censuring of some ministers; the positive work of the Uganda Human Rights Commission and litigation challenging the constitutionality of the referendum law are some of the positive developments on the country's road to constitutionalism.

Frederick W. Jjuuko
Makerere University, Kampala
29 January 2001

Constitutional Development in Kenya

Kivutha Kibwana

Introduction

This report traces and evaluates constitutional developments in Kenya in 1999. It describes the meaning and nature of constitutional development and presents a historical perspective of that development from 1960 to1999. The report then proceeds to describe several issues in constitutional development including the establishment of the process for constitutional change; the constitutional amendment of 1999; the implementation of the constitution; and citizen activism and constitutional development. Lastly, the report discusses the National Convention Executive Council's (NCEC's) attempt to break the constitutional impasse and tackles the emerging issues of constitutional development in Kenya in 1999.

The report reveals that the pre-1999 consensus reached by citizens in entrenching a people-driven process of constitutional review had begun to be reversed in 1999. President Daniel Arap Moi, the ruling Kenya African National Union (KANU) and the co-operating opposition National Development Party (NDP) mounted a vigorous campaign claiming that constitutional reform was the preserve and responsibility of parliament, not civil society. By December 1999, Moi had secured a political strategy for the amendment of the 1998 review law through a parliamentary select committee headed by NDP leader Raila Odinga. In response, civil society and the reform-inclined opposition established the Ufungamano initiative led by religious leaders whose mandate was to make and enforce a people's constitution. Hence, two parallel systems of constitutional review were born in 1999 thereby rendering a trouble-free constitution-making process an impossibility.

The meaning and nature of constitutional development

The present initiative by *Kituo Cha Katiba: East African Centre for Constitutional Development* to annually review the state of constitutional development and thus constitutionalism in East Africa is invaluable for several reasons. For one thing, such assessment is likely to reveal existing shortfalls for corrective action. Also, corresponding strengths can be highlighted and built upon. The evaluation enables each country to monitor its constitutional and democratic record thereby creating an opportunity to incrementally strengthen its culture of constitutionalism. If and when East African countries review their record of constitutionalism annually, will it become possible to compare and borrow best practices in constitutionalism continent-wide. *Kituo's* new effort is thus likely to strengthen constitutionalism in East Africa specifically and even Africa as a whole.

Constitutional development can be examined from several perspectives. Whenever a country makes a new constitution, one can analyse all the processes and activities which feed into and shape such constitution-making. Secondly, constitutional development concerns the way in which the citizens relate to a new or existing constitution. Those activities accompanying the changing or amendment of a constitution similarly provide another aspect of constitutional development. The other key component concerns the implementation of the existing constitution by the executive, judiciary and also the legislature.

A close examination of constitutional development will then crucially show the extent to which a country's citizens and officials collectively make and embrace constitutional norms. The tendency in Africa, however, has been to depart from the official elite-made constitution. Elsewhere I have summarised this trend as follows:

> It is clear to me that in any African country at any given time more than one constitution may be in place. The written or textual constitution is also the aspirational constitution. Opposition leaders or elements and the citizens may clamour for the primacy of such constitution. The political incumbency often claims to follow such a constitution - sometimes even to the letter - but that is usually in rhetoric, or at best the leadership selectively abides by certain parts of the written constitution. Where it is obvious that the leadership feels frustrated by certain sections of the constitution and there is pressure or expectation for these to be followed, then amendments are engineered. These formal amendments are undertaken so that the leadership can continue to argue that it is still faithful to the original constitution or a citizens' derived constituion.[1]

This survey of Kenya's constitutional development also examines the extent to which the legal constitution was adhered to in 1999. Finally, in our analysis of constitutional development, we must also examine whether non-state actors conduct their own affairs through official constitutional norms. This is an important area of enquiry because non-state actors who insist that the state should act constitutionally and democratically must themselves practise constitutionalism.

Constitutional development in historical perspective
1960 - 99[2]

Since this 1999 report on Kenya's constitutional development is the first in *Kituo's* series, a summary of significant constitutional and political developments in the period 1960 - 1998 is imperative. The major highlights of the developments before 1999 are as follows:

1960, 1962 and 1963: Lancaster House constitutional conferences were held in London and Nairobi (1963) to negotiate Kenya's independence constitution.

1963: May elections were held on the principle of one person, one vote. The Kenya National African Union (KANU) emerged victorious. On 1 June the country attained internal self government. On 12 December, full independence was granted.

1963 - 1968: Secession threat by Kenyan Somalis led to protracted civil war and the promulgation of emergency law until 1992. For practical purposes, the North Eastern Province has been run by the government as an occupied territory during war time.

1964: Kenya became a republic and Jomo Kenyatta the president after unification of the hitherto dual executive. KANU and the opposition Kenya African Democratic Union (KADU) merged to pave way for a *de facto* one party system. Various constitutional amendments were effected. The first set (1964 - 88) dismantled multipartyism. The second set (1990 to the present) has begun to hesitantly recreate a multiparty democracy.

1965, 1969, 1975, 1990, 1996: Assassinations of Pio Gama Pinto, Thomas J. Mboya, J.M. Kariuki, Robert Ouko and Karimi Nduthu respectively.

1966: An opposition party, the Kenya Peoples' Union (KPU), was formed.

1969: KPU was banned and its leaders detained.

1969, 1974, 1979, 1983, 1988, 1992, 1997: General elections held.

1978: Jomo Kenyatta died, and his vice president, Daniel Arap Moi, succeeded him as president.

1982: A constitutional amendment made Kenya a *de jure* one party state to forestall the registration of an opposition political party by Jaramogi Oginga Odinga and George Moseti Anyona. In August, there was an attempted military *coup d'etat* which was ruthlessly crushed.

1982 - 88: Protracted crackdown of Mwakenya and other political dissidents. These years represent the heyday of the Moi dictatorship.

1990: *Saba Saba* demonstrations whose central demand was resumption of multipartyism were violently broken up by the police. Scores of demonstrators were killed. KANU established a review committee to collect views from Kenyans on how KANU should be reformed.

1991 - 93: Politically instigated ethnic clashes left about 1,000 Kenyans dead and many thousands more, especially from the major ethnic Kikuyu community, rendered internal refugees.

1991: Donors withdrew budgetary support so as to pressurise for return to multipartyism.

1991: Multipartyism restored through the repeal of section 2A of the constitution.

1995: On New Year's eve, Moi promised that a constitutional review would start.

1996: The National Convention Planning Committee (NCPC), the executive arm of pro-democracy forces who had come together to agitate for constitutional change was formed.

1997: The National Convention Assembly and its executive arm the National Convention Executive Council (NCEC) was formed. Between May and July, widespread mass action forced the government to concede to minimum constitutional and legal changes necessary to facilitate freer and fairer elections. The Constitution of Kenya Review Commission Act, 1997 was passed to provide a framework for constitutional change.

1997-98: Second generation of politically-instigated ethnic clashes.

1998: Negotiations between civil society and the political class for the review of the Constitution of Kenya Review Commission Act, 1997 led to an extensive amendment of the Act via the Constitution of Kenya Review Commission (Amendment) Act 1998 (the amended law was now called the Constitution of Kenya Review Act, 1997) and the creation of a substantially people driven process of constitution-making.

1999: KANU frustrated the establishment of organs for the review of the constitution and therefore the implementation of the review law.

KANU and NDP successfully sponsored a parliamentary motion to facilitate the amendment of the Constitution of Kenya Review Act, 1997.

NCEC launched *Katiba Mpya-Maisha Mpya*: A Vision for National Renewal, a document which detailed how Kenya could overcome the existing political stalemate.

The Ufungamano initiative, a citizen's lobby on constitutional change led by the religious sector, was established with the mandate to facilitate the making of a constitution for Kenyans.

Constitutional developments in 1999

Establishing the process of constitutional change
President Daniel Arap Moi assented to the Constitution of Kenya Review Commission (Amendment) Act, 1998 on 24 December 1998. The law's commencement date was 30 December 1998. Section 4 (1) of the Constitution of Kenya Review Act, 1997[3] provided:

> Within fifteen days of the commencement of this Act, the bodies referred to in sub-section (2) of section 3 shall submit to the Attorney General the names of the persons nominated in accordance with that section for appointment as commissioners.

Section 3 (2) established the constitutional commission to consist of:

- The chairperson;
- Thirteen persons nominated by the political parties as represented in the Interparties Parliamentary Committee of whom at least two shall be women;

- One person nominated by the Kenya Espicopal Conference of Bishops
- One person nominated by the Muslim Consultative Council and the Supreme Council of Kenya Muslims;
- One person nominated by the Protestant churches in Kenya as represented by:
  i. The National Council of Churches of Kenya
  ii. The Seventh Day Adventist Church
  iii. The Church of God
  iv. The Kenya Indigenous Christian Churches
  v. The Evangelical Fellowship of Kenya;
- Five persons nominated by women's organisations through the Kenya Women's Political Caucus of whom at least one shall be a woman with disability;
- Four persons nominated by civil society through the National Council of Non-Governmental Organisations, with particular regard to the youth, the disabled, professional associations and the pastoralists in Kenya, of whom at least one shall be a person with disability and one a woman, and
- The Attorney General or his representative who shall be an ex officio commissioner.

During the third Safari Park forum held to negotiate the amendment of the initial Constitution of Kenya Review Commission Act, 1997, KANU argued it was not necessary to specify the number of commissioners each parliamentary political party was entitled to nominate since the Inter Parties Parliamentary Committee (IPPC) would settle the issue. However, informally agreement was reached on how the 13 seats reserved for parliamentary political parties would be shared.

When the parliamentary parties eventually sat to dispose of the issue, no agreement was reached. In January, they twice failed to agree and, similarly, on 4, 5 and 19 February.[4] On 19 February, KANU even sent 22 representatives to the meeting which was co-ordinating the establishment of the commission instead of two. Further meetings, convened on 22 March and 14 April, did not yield consensus on the selection of political parties nominee commissioners.

The Protestant churches as well as the Kenya Women's Political Caucus supplied two sets of commissioners each to the attorney general. The selection of nominee commissioners by the National Council of Non-Governmental Organisations was also marred by rigging of the elections when one faction of the electorate colluded with the Ministry of Culture and Social Services to register civil society groups which instantly became eligible voters.

Due to the manipulations described above, the commission was never established and thus the constitutional review process could not start.

Although a suit by the *bona fide* officials of the Women's Political Caucus resolved the nomination issue for the caucus,[5] other stage managed stalemates in the nomination process obstructed the establishment of the commission.

Although the 1998 Constitution of Kenya Review Commission (Amendment) Act was largely viewed by the stakeholders who negotiated it as satisfying the criteria of a people-driven process of constitutional change,[6] the National Convention Executive Council identified fifty flaws which rendered the law difficult to implement.[7] Three broad positions were developed over time in relation to whether the review law as amended by the 1998 Act should be amended further or operationalised as it was.

These were:

- According to KANU and NDP, the Act had to be amended to give parliament supreme control over the constitutional review process.
- The non KANU-NDP political parties and civil society groups which had the right to nominate commissioners wanted the Act to be immediately operationalised.
- NCEC called for further amendments to the Act to secure a people's constitution making process further although it recognised that the said Act represented the then highest level of national consensus on how the constitution should be changed.

After effectively frustrating the establishment of the commission, Moi and KANU resumed the boisterous campaign that the proper forum for constitutional reform was parliament because, according to Moi, the process under the review law would cost colossal sums of money and 'Wanjiku' – a euphemism for the ordinary Kenyan who supposedly did not know what the constitution entailed – could not therefore participate in its making. A KANU parliamentary caucus meeting in October resolved to seek parliamentary changes to the 1998 review law to exclude civil society involvement in the organs of constitutional review.

In November and December, a campaign was intensified to amend the 1998 Constitution of Kenya Review Commission (Amendment) Act. A parliamentary select committee was established ostensibly with the mandate to break the stalemate on constitutional review. This committee was dominated by both KANU and NDP.[8] Fifty-four non-NDP opposition MPs led by the Democratic Party (DP) had previously boycotted the proceedings of parliament during the deliberations on the establishment of the parliamentary select committee.

A spirited attempt by Moi to lobby opposition leaders to embrace the route of parliamentary review of the constitution failed before the *fait accompli* passage of the National Assembly's resolution establishing a select committee on 15 December. That resolution stated:

> That while noting that the Constitution of Kenya Review Commission (Amendment) Act 1998 received Presidential Assent on December 24, 1998, with a commencement date of December 30, 1998; cognisant of the fact that the implementation of the Act has been hampered by the disagreement over the nomination of commissioners among some stakeholders, and concerned that the review process is now behind schedule as a result of the impasse; [9] and in order to facilitate consensus building necessary to resolve the stalemate amongst the bodies specified in the First schedule to the Act, the formation of a Review commission and the co-ordination of the constitutional review process, this House resolves to establish a select committee comprising 27 members to review the Constitution of Kenya Review Act according to the wishes of Kenyans and facilitate the formation of the Review Commission.

With the exception of three parliamentarians, the non-KANU-NDP MPs, boycotted the proceedings of the select committee. On 17 December, the chairman of the select committee, Raila Odinga, announced that his committee would meet Kenyans and foreign experts to solicit their opinions on the review.

From the above account it is clear that:

- By the end of 1999 a people-driven process of constitution making which had been agreed on, though imperfect, was about to be dismantled by parliament. However, there was no consensus among the MPs on the move.
- KANU had appeared to support the Constitution of Kenya Review Commission (Amendment) Act, 1998 since in that year it lacked the political strength to oppose or scuttle it. However, KANU's negotiations at Safari Park were not *bona fide*. Indeed, even at the Safari Park forum, KANU's position was that only parliament should review the constitution.
- Through the attorney general's office and some members of the Safari Park Drafting Committee, KANU ensured that the 1998 law was written sloppily rendering it difficult to implement.
- The manner in which the commissioners were allocated especially among civil society – both secular and religious - created divisions in

that progressive segments of civil society were excluded from the commission. Opportunistic elements who had played a minor or no role at all in the struggle for the new constitution ended up in the abortive commission. Acrimony was thereby sowed in civil society.

- It is clear the elite has not developed a consensus on the need for and the scope of constitutional change.
- KANU supports minor changes while other forces support more basic or fundamental changes aimed at undoing dictatorship or cosmetic multipartyism.

If 1997 was a crucial year in the agitation for constitutional change, and 1998 the year of negotiations, 1999 was the year of stalemate; a low point in Kenya's journey towards democratic renewal.

Constitutional amendment in 1999

Towards the end of 1999, curiously a bi-partisan movement to change one aspect of the constitution developed. Initially, KANU appeared to resist it only to embrace it in no time. Assisted by a non-governmental organisation called Centre for Governance and Development (CGD), opposition MP Peter Oloo Aringo introduced a private member's bill whose objective was to amend the constitution in order to enhance the independence of parliament. The bill sought to establish an independent parliamentary service commission.[10] Hitherto parliamentary staff came under the ambit of the Public Service Commission. Moi suggested to KANU that his party should defeat Aringo's bill and then table a similar bill six months later. Twenty five KANU MPs, who apparently disagreed with their chairman and president vowed to support Aringo's bill. Subsequently, however, the government took over the bill which was unanimously passed on 11 November.

Although the above bill appeared to be an opposition initiative, KANU did not ultimately object to it for various reasons. These are:

- Passage of the constitutional amendment by parliament strengthened KANU's argument that only parliament should review the constitution;
- KANU wanted parliament to feel it was independent and should assert itself over civil society although KANU-NDP still controlled parliament;
- A parliamentary service commission alone could not guarantee the independence of parliament because other factors that promoted its subservience to the executive such as constituency gerrymandering, independence of the electoral commission, etc. were not dealt with.

NCEC and the civil society generally criticised the lone amendment on the basis that it was undertaken without consultation with the people of Kenya and gave the impression that parliament was only concerned with those amendments which favoured it as an institution.

Implementation of the constitution

There are several key questions regarding the constitution's implementation which hitherto have not been resolved by legislative intervention or judicial interpretation. They were not also resolved in 1999.

Section 9 (1) provides that the president shall hold office for a term of five years beginning from the date on which he is sworn in as president. (2) No person shall be elected to hold office as president for more than two terms. Does this mean that if a president holds office for less than 5 years, has he/she served a term?

According to section 16 (1) the office of a minister of the government of Kenya shall be established by parliament or, subject to any provisions made by parliament, by the president. Since parliament has never passed such a law, what is the status of the current ministries?

Section 16 (2) provides that the president shall, subject to the provisions of any written law, appoint ministers from among the members of the National Assembly. Such enabling law is yet to be passed.

Presumably the law in question could provide that the president can appoint ministers outside the National Assembly as well and that assembly could vet the president's ministerial nominations. The 1997 amendment of this section which added the language 'subject to the provisions of any written law' is yet to be exploited.

Section 33 (3) provides that nominated MPs shall be nominated by the parliamentary parties according to the proportion of every parliamentary party in the National Assembly, taking into account the principle of gender equality. The judiciary is yet to interpret what 'taking into account the principle of gender equality' actually means. Section 47 provides for the alteration of the constitution. The courts have not yet interpreted whether this includes *de novo* constitution making.

According to section 61(2) puisne judges shall be appointed by the president acting in accordance with the advice of the Judicial Service Commission. The judiciary has not yet been moved to determine whether persons appointed as judges without the advice of the Judicial Service Commission are legally appointed.

Section 84 (5) provides:

Parliament (a) may confer upon the High Court such powers in addition to those conferred by this section as may appear to be necessary or desirable for the purpose of enabling that court, more effectively to exercise the jurisdiction conferred upon it by this section; and

(b) shall make provision for -

(i) rendering of financial assistance to any indigent citizen of Kenya where his right under this chapter (Chapter V) has been infringed or with a view to enabling him engage the services of an advocate to prosecute his claim; and

(ii)ensuring that allegations of infringement of such rights are substantial and the requirement or need for financial or legal aid is real.

Parliament is yet to pass a law to implement this constitutional provision.

Under section 84 (6) the chief justice is empowered to make rules with respect to the practice and procedure of the High Court in relation to the vindication of human rights. The chief justice has never made such rules.

According to sections 115, 117 and 118, trust land cannot be alienated to those it is not held in trust for unless it is first set apart. Since independence substantial land has been alienated in contravention of the constitution. No court has conclusively interpreted these provisions.

Some areas in which the executive acted in support of the constitution in 1999 are the following:

- In January the minister in charge of agriculture sacked the entire National Irrigation Board after farmers' riots which had challenged its management.
- In March, the executive pressurised the board of the National Bank of Kenya to take responsibility for massive bad loans and thereby resign. The government had 22.5 per cent shares in the bank and a public parastatal the National Social Security Fund (NSSF) had 37.5 per cent shares in the bank. The government seemed interested in sending a signal that it was protecting public property.
- In April, the president finally appointed a vice president after 14 months of the position being vacant.
- In July, the president appointed the so-called *dream team* consisting of technocrats sourced from the private sector and multilateral organisations. Their mandate was to clean the civil service and revive the economy.
- In July, the president placed a ban on the allocation of land until further notice. This was as a consequence of public protest against illegal allocation of such land and public forests.

- In September, the president reduced the number of ministries from 27 to 15 but retained the 27 ministers so that most of the ministries are led by several ministers.

Several cases of constitutional significance were lodged in court. In February, the Law Society of Kenya sued the chief justice requiring him to establish a tribunal to investigate bribery allegations against High Court Judge Richard Kuloba under section 62 of the constitution.[11] In February also, the president was sued for the second time for not appointing a vice president.[12] The suit by the Supreme Council of Kenya Muslims enjoined the attorney general whom it accused of failing to advise the president appropriately on the matter.

In September, Nairobi Town Clerk Zipporah Wandera was jailed for contempt of court. She had defied a court order of 25 June nullifying the Nairobi City Council decision to prevent Qurdoba Enterprises from distributing petrol in Nairobi. Her activity was viewed, *inter alia*, as a violation of the constitutionally protected property rights of Qurdoba Enterprises.[13] In September, a new chief justice who had previously been a pro-government prosecutor, famous for prosecuting human rights and pro-democracy activists, was appointed. The Law Society of Kenya unsuccessfully opposed his elevation.[14] The February cases were never concluded in the plaintiffs' favour.

It is clear from this segment that both the executive and the judiciary have not actively safeguarded the constitution and promoted democratic changes.

Citizen activism and constitutional development

In the first part of the year, many citizens and their groups were involved in activism which impacted on constitutional development:

- In January, two women were arrested in a demonstration protesting the allocation of the Nakuru Municipality Retail Market to a private developer. Traders demolished a fast food facility erected in the same market.
- In January, rice farmers in Kirinyaga and Mwea protested against the manner in which the National Irrigation Board handled their affairs. One farmer was shot dead.
- In February students of University of Nairobi rioted over the illegal allocation by government of Karura forest to private individuals.
- In March, riots broke out in Nyeri and Karatina, Central Province in which citizens were protesting the poor state of roads. Also in Kisumu

Jua Kali traders protested the demolition of their kiosks by the municipal council.

- In March, inter-denominational prayers were held in Nairobi to protest the allocation of Karura forest to private developers.
- On 11 March, NCEC relaunched a reform movement to agitate for constitutional reform.
- In April, mourners protesting the killing of the chairman of the Kamae squatters Resettlement Scheme carried his casket to the chief's camp, blaming his death on the government.
- In June, a Budget Day demonstration for an all inclusive process of constitutional change was violently broken outside parliament. PCEA clergyman Rev. Timothy Njoya and NCEC co-convenor Davinder Lamba were injured.
- In June, a strike against the Transport Licensing Board rules was staged by the Matatu transport sector. The said rules sought to phase out tout operators and to replace them with city council workers.
- A rally held to commemorate *Saba Saba* Day in July called on Kenyans to force Moi out of office.
- In July, Nairobi City Council workers held a strike to demand salary arrears.
- On 21 September, Catholic bishops demanded a peoples' process of constitutional change. The 15 bishops and 2 priests met the president at State House.
- On 26 September, the Catholic church launched civic education materials to prepare Kenyans for constitutional review. Archbishop Ndingi Mwanaa Nzeki warned that dictators will not be allowed to derail the process.
- On 30 September, 23 Catholic bishops warned the country's leadership that civil strife was imminent if the several crises facing the country were not addressed. In their pastoral letter they identified the key problems as corruption, hunger, plunder of public resources, HIV/AIDS, insecurity and collapsed infrastructure.
- On 17 October, Catholic bishops began another round of protests over the review process with an open mass at the Holy Family Minor Basilica, Nairobi.
- On 21 October, religious leaders united in condemning KANU's proposal that civil society be excluded from the review process. They demanded that the attorney general reconvenes the Safari Park forum so that it could oversee the nomination of commissioners; that the 1998 review law should not be taken back to parliament; and that all

the stakeholders named in the Act must participate in constitution - making.

- On 3 December, religious leaders announced their intention to call a meeting of all stakeholders at Ufungamano House.
- On 15 December, the Ufungamano initiative was established with the mandate that it should write a people's constitution for Kenya.

In 1999 Kenyans were engaged in various protests and other activities which had constitutional implications. Also the religious fraternity accepted for the first time to lead the constitutional reform process. However, the religious sector may not have been prepared to lead citizens in preparing a new constitution but rather in renegotiations to amend the Constitution of Kenya Review Commission (Amendment) Act, 1998 to facilitate the onset of *bona fide* constitutional review. A bigger responsibility than the religious leaders had anticipated was suddenly thrust on them.

NCEC's attempt to break the constitutional impasse

In November, NCEC launched an important document which it hoped would form the basis for national discussion on how to overcome the country's political stalemate.[15] The NCEC's National Rescue Action Plan was predicated, inter alia, on:

> a unified movement of all democratic forces (since) to work for the salvation of the nation rather than for limited political goals, we need a movement of people from all ethnic groups, all religious faiths, all occupations and all democratic political positions working together in solidarity.[16]

The Action Plan[17] consisted of six key steps, that is:
(i) Breaking the current stalemate over constitutional reform through the establishment of a self-governing multisectoral forum which would:

- (a) renegotiate the Constitution of Kenya Review Act, 1997 fix the flaws in the Act and make the review process workable and democratic.
- (b) negotiate the formation of a neutral transition institution to act as a caretaker government during the period of constitutional review.
- (c) negotiate a transitional justice mechanism to grant immunity from prosecution persons who may have committed political crimes in the past.

(d) negotiate a package of interim democratic reforms to enable Kenyans participate freely in constitutional review.

(e) play the role of 'citizen's watchdog' throughout the period of constitutional review.

(ii) Set up a caretaker government which is fully representative and competent to govern. Such caretaker government would:

(a) pass the interim constitutional reforms negotiated by the multisectoral forum;

(b) implement the transitional justice programme;

(c) the multisectoral forum's interim democratic reforms agenda;

(d) the multisectoral forum's economic recovery programme; and

(e) safeguard the constitutional review process negotiated by the multisectoral forum.

(iii) Implementing the interim democratic reforms programme.

(iv) Implementing an interim economic and social recovery programme

(v) Creating a new constitution.

(vi) Ratifying the new constitution and inaugurating a new democratic order.

Although the media sensationalised the Action Plan by claiming that the NCEC had called for a military government,[18] the proposals for breaking Kenya's political stalemate in 1999 were perhaps the most well thought out. If implemented, those proposals had the potential of securing Kenya's democratic transition.

Conclusion: Emerging issues in constitutional development in 1999

Several important themes or issues emerge from the 1999 survey of constitutional development in Kenya. The government felt it was in a strong position to reverse the citizen gains of 1997 and 1998 secured through passage of the Inter Parties Parliamentary Group reforms[19] and the Constitution of Kenya Review Commission (Amendment) Act, 1998. Increasingly government adopted a lukewarm attitude towards the implementation of the IPPG reforms. Further, government demonstrated it. had no interest in implementing the 1998 law to pave way for bona fide constitutional review. Government sought to replace the negotiated people driven process of constitutional review with a parliamentary driven one captured by KANU. Government in 1999 employed every trick to stall the momentum of constitutional reform. The objective, as had been the case since 1990, was to delay the onset of constitution-making thereby ensuring the continuation of a one party inspired constitution within a multiparty era. Ninenteen ninety nine ended on a sad note for constitutional development in Kenya because the government had by the end of that year confined constitutional debate at the level of process, not content. Thus, 1999 closed the decade of the 1990s by confirming that Kenya's ruling elite had never embraced broad-based constitution-making. Indeed, all along the government had preferred and advocated piecemeal constitutional amendments, not overhaul.

The executive also continued to show it lacked fidelity to constitutionalism. A good example was the president's refusal to appoint a vice president when the language of the constitution on that appointment is mandatory.

KANU, which clearly showed that it was not prepared to respect any negotiations that did not suit its interests was determined to reverse the Constitution of Kenya Review Commission (Amendment) Act, 1998. This KANU attitude makes future negotiations problematic since that party has demonstrated that it cannot honour its commitments unless they suit its interests as happened in relation to the constitutional establishment of the Parliamentary Service Commission.

Critically, in 1999, it was also demonstrated that Kenya's citizens and generally the secular and religious civil society are significantly interested in participating in the constitutional and democratic rebirth of that country. The question of constitutional reengineering is no longer a concern of only the political elite.

Even grassroots populations are involved in activism geared at expanding their constitutional gains and getting a foothold in a people-driven process of constitution-making. At the close of the year, two competing processes of constitution-making – a parliamentary-driven process, and a people-driven process led by the religious sector – were unfolding. President Moi and KANU had not, therefore, won a victory over Kenyans on the way the constitution would be written. The stage was set for further contest between the people and the KANU regime in 2000 on who will have the last word on constitution-making. Fortunately, history reveals that ultimately the people must triumph.

Notes

1. As amended by the Constitution of Kenya Review Commission (Amendment) Act, 1998, 38:42.

2. For information in this section, I relied on Kivutha Kibwana (with assistance from Jelvas Musau and Antony Munene) 'Kenya' in Christof Heyns (Ed.), *Human Rights Law in Africa 1997*, The Hague, London, Boston, 1999:180 - 85.

3. As amended by the Constitution of Kenya Review Commission (Amendment) Act, 1998.

4. See the *Daily Nation* January - December 1999 for all the factual accounts in this segment.

5. *Ibid,* 4 February at 2.

6. See Generally, Kivutha Kibwana, 'Weaknesses in the constitution of Kenya Review Act, 1997,' Centre for Law and Research International, Mimeo, March 1999.

7. *Ibid.*

8. See Republic of Kenya, National Assembly Eighth Parliament - Fourth Session, Report of theParliamentary Select Committee Reviewing the Constitution of Kenya Review Act, 1997, Nairobi April 2000 at 1 - 2.

9. *Ibid* at 1.

10. See the Parliamentary Service Commission Bill, 1999. See also Daily Nation, 12 November at 1.

11. *Daily Nation,* February 10 at 1.

12. *Ibid,* 24 February at 1.

13. *Ibid,* 29 September at 1.

14. *Ibid,* 14 September at 1.

15. See NCEC, *Katiba Mpya - Maisha Mpya*: A vision for National Renewal, Nairobi., NCEC, 1999

16. *Ibid* at 17.

17. The rest of this account is closely based on *Ibid* 17 - 35

18. *Daily Nation*, 8 November at 1.

19. See The Constitution of Kenya (Amendment) Act, 1997 and the Statute Law (Repeals and Miscellaneous Amendments) Act, 1997 Kenya Gazette Supplement No. 70 (Acts No. 7) at 843 - 913.

Constitution-making in Tanzania: The Role of Civil Society Organisations

Chris Maina Peter

No one person has the right to say, "I am the People." No Tanzanian has the right to say, "I know what is good for Tanzania and others must do it." All Tanzanians have to make the decisions for Tanzania.

Julius Kambarage Nyerere[1].

Introduction: The constitution and constitution-making

The constitution of a country is the most important legal document. It is the supreme law on which all other laws are based. At times it is called a social contract between the rulers and the ruled. It also represents the consensus amongst the people themselves. The constitution is therefore more than just a document. It embodies the wishes and aspirations of the country. All the laws, by-laws, rules and regulations derive their legitimacy from the constitution.

Constitutions take various forms. There are written and unwritten constitutions. Great Britain, for instance, has no written constitution. It is guided by traditions developed over the years. However, most countries and particularly those in the developing world have written constitutions. Most of these constitutions have been developed and shaped by their colonial past. Some were negotiated with the departing colonial powers. They were or are compromises between the interests of the colonial rulers and the ruled who were taking over power. Yet others are outcomes of protracted independence struggle – mostly armed.

Some of these developing countries have gone beyond the so-called independence constitutions to home-grown constitutions. They have nevertheless retained the tradition of the former rulers. For instance, constitutions of most the former British colonies retained the Westminster tradition with a clear separation of powers, independence of the judiciary and generally the existence of checks and balances. Others have tilted the balance in favour of a strong executive and a very weak judiciary and a rubber-stamping legislature.

This paper examines the role played by the people in the constitution-making process in Tanzania. The work begins by examining the struggle for independence and the movement towards the very first constitution of the country – the independence constitution of 1961.

Later on we look at the process of constitution making after independence. The focal point is the role of the people in this process. This area covers struggles of over thirty years. We conclude by a prognosis on what the future holds for the people of Tanzania in the process of constitution making for the country.

Struggle for independence: The role played by the people through civic organisations

Tanzania was formally under the British as a mandate under the League of Nations and later as a trustee territory under the United Nations.[2] Its independence constitution was negotiated with the former rulers. In these negotiations the departing British had an upper hand. The nationalists and the people, on the other hand, did not have a clear say in the process of framing the independence constitution. One known concession made by the British allowed Tanganyika to become independent with a constitution that did not contain a bill of rights.[3] That was important as far as the nationalists were concerned because they no longer had a duty to protect the properties of the subjects of the departing rulers.

During the struggle for independence, and particularly in the 1940s and 1950s, there was a very close relationship between the nationalist leaders and their people organised in civic organisations which the colonial regime allowed to exist. It was almost impossible to separate the politicians and these civic groups.[4]

The peasants in their co-operative movements and the working people in their various trade unions provided the nationalist leaders with a forum through which they could address the public 'legally' without having to go through the rigours of getting the required permits for meetings from the authorities. It is on record that even social organisations of the people such as football clubs like *Young Africans Sports Club* popularly known as *Yanga* and Taarab Clubs such as *Egyptian Musical Club* in Dar es Salaam were civil groups which assisted the nationalist movement in its struggle for the independence of the country.

Therefore, the role of the people during the colonial period cannot be underestimated. They were very effective in their various organisations. Worth noting, as indicated above, were the co-operative movement and the trade unions. This very amicable and supportive relationship was to change very much after independence.

Independence and the parting of company between the leaders and the led

At independence the very close relationship between the politicians and the people in their various organisations gradually came to an end. This was due to the differences in perception of what political independence meant for the people of Tanzania. As for the co-operative movement things were much easier. The top brass in the major co-operative societies were co-opted easily into the new government. In the forefront were the leaders of co-operative societies from the Lake Victoria area such as Paul Bomani from Victoria Federation in Mwanza, a strong cotton growing zone and George Kahama from Bukoba which was a strong coffee growing area. This co-option did not mean freedom for the co-operative movement. It was (and still is) placed under the tight control of the government with the minister responsible for Agriculture keeping an open eye on their operations.[5]

The problem was the trade unions. There was a sharp division and divergence of views among the leadership. Some wanted to join the new government and get into politics proper. Others wanted to maintain their positions in the trade unions and continue with the struggle for the improvement of the welfare of the working people. Yet others joined the government for a short while and later left. There were serious repercussions to follow for the trade union movement in the country.[6]

Therefore, people like Michael Kamaliza and Alfred Tandau joined the new government and were given cabinet posts. Other union leaders like Christopher Kasanga Tumbo joined the government for a short time and then left.[8] For those who insisted on continuing the trade union tradition of fighting for the rights and welfare of workers the government was losing patience.[9] The Tanganyika Federation of Labour (TFL) was outlawed and the leadership banished to remote areas of the country. One of the top leaders of the movement, Victor Mkello, was deported to the remote town of Sumbawanga.[9] TFL was replaced by a state-sponsored and supported National Union of Tanzania Workers (NUTA) which was affiliated to the ruling party. For many years to follow, the secretary-general of this 'trade union' was always a cabinet minister responsible for labour. That development marked the end of the struggle over the destiny of the country between the people in their organisations, one the one hand, and the government, on the other.

For most of the post-independence period, the civil society, through which the people were organised and thus could express themselves, was submerged within the ruling party. This was in the form of what was called mass organisations of the ruling party. These were made up of the youth, the parents, the workers, women and peasants (co-operatives).[11] As a result of this co-option by the state, these civil groups could not contribute meaningfully to the advancement of the struggle towards a progressive and democratic country. In terms of constitutional development, it meant that civic groups did not contribute to the betterment of the constitution as the main law of the country governing the relations between people and their government and among themselves.

Major constitutional changes in the country

The major constitutional changes after independence point at one common thing. There was an attempt by the ruling party and its government to show the rest of the world that there was democracy in the country and that the people were fully involved in the constitutional process. That was quite understandable since even the most autocratic system does not own up to being autocratic. And to be democratic or to be seen to be democratic you have to be seen to be consulting the people. That is what has been happening in Tanzania. The party and its government pretended that they were consulting the people – while, in fact, they were not consulting anybody at all.

To prove our assertion, we look at various directions of the constitutional process from independence to the present. We examine the shift from a multi-party to a one-party state; the consolidation of one-party system and the return to multipartyism. We end with an examination of the most recent constitutional amendment – the 13th Amendment of 2000 which followed the controversial White Paper debate.

From multi-party to one-party democracy

Tanzania, then known as Tanganyika, was a vibrant multi-party democracy at independence. The independence constitution of 1961 provided a legal and constitutional framework for that. Apart from the dominant Tanganyika African National Union (TANU), there were two other political parties. These were the United Tanganyika Party (UTP) formed in 1958 and backed by the landed section of white settlers in the country to counter the influence of TANU; and the African National Congress (ANC) which was also formed in 1958 by Zuberi Mtemvu after leaving TANU over disagreements over the position to be taken at elections.

After independence, other parties emerged. These included, the Peoples Democratic Party (PDP) of Christopher Kasanga Tumbo; the Peoples Convention Party (PCP) led by Samson Mshala; the Nationalist Enterprise Party (NEP) of Hussein Yahaya; the All Muslim Nationalist Union of Tanganyika (AMNUT); and the African Independence Movement (AIM) which was a merger between PCP and NEP.[11] In this multiparty democracy, there was a clear consensus that parliament was the supreme organ of the people. This was conceded by the former president of the United Republic of Tanzania, the late Mwalimu Julius K. Nyerere, in a speech made on 25 April 1964 to the National Assembly asking it to ratify the Union between Tanganyika and Zanzibar. In this speech Mwalimu said:

> The Parliament is the supreme organ of the people of Tanganyika. No important constitutional issues or important matter concerning state agreement or concerning the laws of this country, can be finally decided by anyone or any group of persons other than this Assembly. All such matters must be brought before this house, and it is entirely at your discretion to approve them or reject them. Today, I am submitting to you for consideration a draft agreement for the Union of Tanganyika and Zanzibar.[12]

This was to change very soon. First, other political parties had to go in order to pave the way for a on-party political system. According to Professor Cranford Pratt, a Canadian political scientist and the first principal of the University College at Dar es Salaam:

> In Tanzania the several tiny parties which appeared in 1962 were harassed out of existence, their leadership deported or detained and their rights to register and hold meetings severely restricted.[13]

With other parties out of the way, the time was ripe to declare a one-party political system. The argument for this came from the party president himself. In a speech to the TANU national conference in 1963, he argued:

> Where there is one party, and that party is identified with the nation as a whole, the foundations of democracy are firmer than they can ever be where you have two or more parties, each representing only a section of the community.

What followed was a decision of the party's National Executive Committee (NEC) to turn Tanganyika into a one-party state. This party decision was to be given legal backing two years later *vide* the interim constitution of 1965.

There was no attempt to involve the people in the decision-making process. The party had decided for them. Therefore, even when the president of the country formed a commission on the establishment of a one-party state he was very clear on their limited mandate:

In order to avoid misunderstanding, I think I should emphasise that it is not the task of this Commission to consider whether Tanganyika should be a one-party state. The decision has already been taken. Their task is to say what kind of one party state we should have in the context of our own national ethic and in accordance with the principles I have instructed the Commission to observe.[14]

The next step was to declare the sole party supreme. Again, the first person to hint at party supremacy was Mwalimu Nyerere. When conveying fraternal greetings to the conference of the Uganda Peoples Congress (UPC) on 7 June 1968 the president of TANU argued a case for party supremacy very articulately:

For the truth is that it is not the party which is the instrument of the government. It is the government which is the instrument through which the party tries to implement the wishes of the people and serve their interests.[15]

Party supremacy was officially entrenched in the constitution of the country in 1975.[16]

The party leadership at the same time controlled the government. This gave them control over both the ideological and coercive state apparatus. It was the same people making decisions in the party and then overseeing their implementation in the government. Changing hats took place depending on the seat – party president or country president. Already by 1971 the system of checks and balances between the organs of the state had been completely dismantled. Parliament and the judiciary had completely lost the war with the executive. The president was so confident as to tell the British Broadcasting Corporation (BBC) in an interview that 'I have powers under the Constitution to be a dictator.'[17]

The interim constitution of 1965

The interim constitution of the United Republic of Tanzania is taken as the third constitution – following the independence and the republican constitutions of 1961 and 1962 respectively. Its enactment indicates the new power of the single ruling party and total disregard of constitutional process. No constituent assembly was ever convened to pass this constitution. It was adopted by parliament in its constituent capacity as if it was amending an existing constitution.

This constitution recognised the changes brought about by the Union and also adopted most of the proposals made by the One-Party Commission. The most significant was the rejection of a bill of rights and the placing of fundamental rights and freedoms in the preamble. In addition, the constitution of the ruling party TANU was also appended to the national constitution and as such it became part of the supreme law of the country. It is not clear why it was decided to append the constitution of one party only – TANU – and exclude that of the ASP when in fact the two parties existed simultaneously in the country.

It is worth noting that in the process of bringing this new constitution into operation the people had been clearly and deliberately by-passed. No attempt was made to involve them. It was party leaders who were busy preparing documents and using the state machinery to see them through the legal processes in order to avoid criticism. Little effort was taken to ensure the legitimacy of the new constitution.

This constitution was *interim*. According to the articles of the Union of Zanzibar and Tanganyika of 1964, a new permanent constitution was supposed to be adopted within *one year* after the commencement of the Union.[18] This time frame was extended almost indefinitely and the interim constitution was to last for twelve years until the permanent constitution was eventually adopted in 1977.[19]

The permanent constitution of the United Republic of Tanzania of 1977

On 5 February 1977, the two existing political parties in the country – Tanganyika African National Union (TANU) and Afro Shirazi Party (ASP) – merged to form *Chama Cha Mapinduzi* (CCM). This new party was proclaimed at Amani Stadium in Zanzibar, following the approval by the joint general congress of TANU and ASP on 21 January 1977.

What is interesting is the fact that it is the same committee which had been appointed back in October 1976 to prepare a constitution for a new party which was assigned to prepare the new constitution for the country. On 16 March 1977, the president of the United Republic of Tanzania appointed this 20-person committee headed by the late Thabit Kombo to make proposals for a constitution for the United Republic.[20]

Strangely, on the same date, i.e. 16 March 1977, the president appointed and summoned the Constituent Assembly to discuss and enact the new constitution of the United Republic.[21] According to Professor Issa G. Shivji:

> The Commission had started working on the Constitution even before it was formally appointed as the Constitution Commission. It submitted its proposals to the National Executive Committee [of the new Party CCM] which adopted them in camera in a one day meeting. These proposals were then published in the form of a Bill and within seven days submitted to the Constituent Assembly. The Constituent Assembly passed the new Constitution within three hours.[22]

Thus, in the making of this constitution there was no consultation or debate. Everything was forced through by the powerful ruling party. Yet this was the permanent constitution of the country.

The 1983 constitutional debate

Notwithstanding the tight grip of the party over the country and the gradual curtailing of the various rights and freedoms, the members of the public never gave up their right to contribute to the welfare of their society. Whenever an opportunity offered itself the public tended to grab and utilise it to the full.

One such opportunity came when the ruling party tried to effect changes to the constitution of the United Republic of Tanzania of 1977 in 1983. There was a serious debate on the constitution and the people almost hijacked it and contributed effectively to this debate. The ruling party, being supreme under the constitution, declared the areas it wanted to be changed. These areas were:

1. The powers of the president;
2. Consolidation of the authority of parliament;
3. Strengthening the representative character of the National Assembly;
4. Consolidation of the Union; and
5. Consolidation of the peoples power.[23]

Due to the long suppression under one-party rule, the debate began slowly with the people, wanting to remain within the dictates of the party. That is, to restrict their views only to the areas decreed by the party. However, as the debate gathered tempo, members of the public began making comments on the whole constitution and indicating various weaknesses in the instrument.[24]

Leading in this crusade was the society of advocates and lawyers in the country, the Tanganyika Law Society (TLS). This society has a long and chequered history. Over the years, it has evolved from a conservative lawyers' club to a force to reckon with on constitutional issues. According to Tambila:

> Most NGOs, as part of Tanzanian civil society, kept a very low profile during the years of demobilisation of civil society with the notable exceptions of Tanganyika Law Society, the University of Dar es Salaam Academic Staff Assembly (UDASA) and CHAKIWATA[25]. From 1983 the Tanganyika Law Society became very vocal on issues concerning the Constitution and actually led the debate on democracy in the late 1980s and early 1990s.[26]

Therefore, whenever the issue of the rights of the citizens has been placed on the agenda, the society has been very clear in expressing the views of the majority of its members. For instance, when the president appointed the Commission on the One-Party State which went around the country collecting people's views, TLS sent a well considered memorandum to that commission arguing that it was necessary to have a bill of rights in the constitution of the country to make that constitution respectable to the members of the international community.[27] The recommendation was ignored by the commission but the point had been made.

The 1983 debate was another opportunity for the Law Society to make its mark on the constitutional map of the country. As the debate progressed, the society organised a three-day seminar on the constitution. Among the contributors to this seminar was Wolfgang Dourado, the former attorney-general of Zanzibar, who wrote a paper on the union between Tanganyika and Zanzibar advocating a three-government system instead of the current two. During the seminar, participants openly argued for an introduction of multi-party democracy to replace the one-party system and party supremacy. It was also insisted that the time had come for the bill of rights to be entrenched into the constitution of the country. Also, participants argued that those who did not belong to CCM should be allowed to form their own political parties or join political parties of their own choice.

The government of the day was not happy with the issues raised in the seminar. While closing the seminar, Joseph Warioba, the then attorney-general and minister for Justice, clearly reminded the lawyers that it was important to adhere to the party guidance on the areas which required changes in the constitution.

This seminar had two opposite results–one positive and the other negative. On the positive side, the seminar opened the way for the incorporation of a bill of rights into the constitution of the United Republic of Tanzania of 1977.[28] This is because the lawyers at the seminar were able to articulate and crystallise the wishes of the majority of the people of Tanzania as expressed in various fora in a variety of ways. Interestingly, the question of incorporating a bill of rights in the constitution was outside the purview of the five issues decreed by the ruling party as open for debate. On the negative side, two of the ideas raised and developed in the course of the seminar were summarily rejected. These were those on the introduction of a multi-party political system in the country and re-organisation of the two-government union into a three-government federation. To add salt to the injury, Wolfgang Dourado, one of the proponents of these ideas, was detained under the 1992 Preventive

Detention Act immediately after the seminar. He spent over a hundred days in custody. This detention was triggered by what he said in his paper at the seminar.[29]

Nevertheless, the fact that a bill of rights incorporated into the constitution of Tanzania boosted the morale of not only the lawyers in the society, but also the members of the public and the NGO fraternity. It demonstrated that with spirited and concerted efforts, members of the public could effect change in the constitution and other areas of public life affecting their daily life. The important lesson was that everything had to be fought for inch by inch.

The Nyalali Commission on the one-party vs the multi-party system

The events in 1983 did not deter those who wanted change in the constitution of the country from continuing their agitation for constitutional reform. Whenever an opportunity presented itself, it was thoroughly utilised. At the end of the 1980s, the Eastern bloc of socialist countries was slowly disintegrating. It began with the fall of the formidable Berlin Wall separating East from West Berlin fell leading to the reunification of Germany. This was followed by the collapse of communism and the disintegration of the Union of Soviet Socialist Republics (USSR) into fifteen independent countries.

These changes were well illustrated by Tambila when he wrote:

> External influences included ... the dramatic changes taking place in Eastern Europe and the now defunct Soviet Union, starting with the 1985 accession to power of Mikhail Gorbachev who initiated change and openness under the banner of *perestoika* and *glasnost*. The events included the collapse of the Stalinist regimes in East Germany, Bulgaria and the violent collapse of the communist regime in Rumania; the changes were epitomised by the fall of the Berlin Wall and the ignominious deaths of Nikolae and Yelena Ceaucescu of Rumania.[30]

These and other developments in the world had their effects on democracy and the process of democratisation in Tanzania.

Thus, in 1991 President Ali Hassan Mwinyi appointed a commission under the chairmanship of Justice Francis Nyalali, the then chief justice of Tanzania, to collect the views of the people on what type of political system they would like, that is to choose between one-party and multi-party political systems and advise the government accordingly.[31] The commission was given one year to complete its work.[32]

During the debates introduced by the commission all over the country, lawyers, again in their society, took a central role. The society under the presidency of Bob Makani organised a very successful conference at the Institute of Finance Management hall. Papers on constitutionalism were presented and at the end of the conference the participants 'voted' for a multi-party political system of government.[33] This 'voting' was not well received in the ruling party and government. For example, Rashid Kawawa, the then party secretary-general claimed that the lawyers were about to mislead the people again.

Yet, when the time came to make decisions on the recommendations of the Nyalali Commission, the government adopted the multi-party political system.[34] This is what the Tanganyika Law Society had been advocating over the years. A hard struggle had to be waged for the government to give in to this demand.[35]

The White Paper: The work of the Kisanga Committee

For a long time, the members of the public have been critical of the way the ruling party and its government have been handling changes to the constitution of the country. Since its adoption in 1977, there have been over thirteen amendments touching on various issues. Lawyers and the pro-democracy movement in the country have described these amendments as patches (*viraka*) which have not managed to bring about any serious constitutional reforms. They have maintained and consolidated the *status quo*. This has led over time to agitation for the formulation of a new constitution which will take into account the interests of all stake-holders in the country that is, people from all works of life – peasants, workers, students, religious groups, professionals etc. These interest groups can only be brought together in a national conference to jointly write a completely new social contract to govern the relationship among themselves and with their government.[36]

Instead of addressing the issues being raised, the ruling party has remained adamant. It has argued and continues to argue that the current constitution is both legal and legitimate and therefore the question of writing a new constitution does not arise.

Nevertheless, in order to reduce the mounting pressure, in 1998 the government floated the idea a White Paper[38] on constitutional change. The White Paper is basically a British method seeking to know the views of the public on a particular issue of national importance. It goes hand in hand with what is called a Green Paper. In the Green Paper the government of the day raises issues for public discussion. On receipt of the reactions from the public, the government may add its own views after which it comes out with a White Paper. Therefore, essentially a White Paper contains both the summarised views of the public and those of the government. In Tanzania, the government is fond of copying things half way. Its version of a White Paper was strange. It contained both the issues and the views of the government on those issues. The public was expected to add whatever they considered appropriate for discussion i.e 'any other view.' This was technically to pre-empt debate on these issues.

A committee of 16 members led by Justice Robert Kisanga of the Court of Appeal of Tanzania, and a respectable member of the legal fraternity, was appointed. The committee visited all districts in the country and presented a four-volume report of over 800 pages to the president of the United Republic of Tanzania.

As the report was being presented, the government made it categorically clear that it would disregard those recommendations of the committee which conflicted with the views of the 'people.' This was a strange position because there were precedents of the same government adopting recommendations of past commissions contrary to the views of the 'people.'

The government kept its word, in an unprecedented fashion. Without releasing the report to the public, the president blasted the Kisanga Committee for going beyond its mandate by making recommendations which were contrary to the views of the people [read here views of the government]. On his part, the chairman of the committee retorted that the president was entitled to his own views and could pick whatever he found useful in the report. Accordingly, the whole momentum built through the work of the committee was lost. That meant that another opportunity to meaningfully better the constitution of the country was missed.

Parallel to the Kisanga Committee, the Tanganyika Law Society independently sought the people's views on the constitution. It held public meetings in various parts of the country and people gave their views on what they wanted to see in their constitution. The work of the society was completely ignored by the government. No comment was made on this valuable task and the legislation that followed, including the 13th amendment to the constitution, never referred to the work of TLS.

The 13th amendment to the constitution of April 2000

True to its word, the government prepared the 13th amendment to the constitution of the United Republic of Tanzania[38] on the basis of its own views in the White paper. The amendment has in fact taken the country back instead of advancing the constitutional democratic tradition. A lot of gains that Tanzania made during the 1990s have been lost through this amendment. The following examples clearly illustrate this point.

Firstly, before this amendment, a candidate had to win more than 50 per cent of votes in the presidential elections to be declared president of the ·United Republic. The amendment abolished this requirement. Today, a candidate only needs to win by a *simple majority* to be declared president.[39] According to its sponsors, this amendment was meant to avoid expensive presidential elections re-runs. However, since the president is supposed to be a symbol of the whole country, he should win the support of the majority of the voters and enjoy pan-territorial acceptability. Moreover, the amendment meant that a single ethnic group or merger of related ethnic groups can 'sponsor' a presidential candidate and succeed. The same could be said for a religion. One of the major religions can identify a presidential candidate and 'work' for his or her success in the elections. A president by *simple majority* is a liability rather than a blessing and this is a negative constitutional development in the country.

Secondly, before this amendment, all members of parliament, save for the attorney-general, women in the special seats and those representing the Zanzibar House of Representatives, were directly elected from the constituencies. The president did not have power to nominate anybody to parliament. The 13th amendment has taken Tanzania back to the one-party era when parliament was dominated by those who entered the House through the back door i.e. through nomination or holding certain constitutional offices such as regional commissioners, etc. Now this' amendment allows the president to nominate up to ten members of parliament.[40] As a justification, we are told that this is meant to give the president an opportunity to appoint some 'experts' to parliament. These are 'experts' who shy away from the active competitive politics of elections.

One may wish to note that parliament is a representative body. All citizens cannot sit together to make laws and other rules to regulate their affairs. They have delegated this duty to their representatives in parliament. Members of parliament are supposed to represent their constituents and not to exercise a certain expertise. Therefore, the legitimacy of being in parliament is derived from the concept of the sovereignty of the people. Experts can always be called upon to assist parliament to clarify complicated issues. However, they need not belong to parliament since they represent nobody. If the president is interested in experts, he can always hire them as permanent secretaries, presidential advisers etc. These will be normal bureaucrats doing their duties for the country. Therefore, filling parliament with 'experts' who enter the House by the back door has little logic. It simply gives the executive arm of the government more weight to push convenient or partisan legislation with or without popular support. This was the case in the one-party parliament which had a majority of nominated members. Therefore, to revert back to nominations is definitely retrogressive.

One positive element in the 13th amendment is the increase in the number of special seats for women. The number of MPs in this category will increase from the current 15 percent to 20 percent plus depending on the declaration by the National Electoral Commission from time to time with the consent of the president.[41] This is a welcome development given the small number of female MPs in the current parliament.

Conclusion

From what has been covered above, it is obvious that since independence the people of Tanzania have never been genuinely involved in the constitution-making process. The half-hearted efforts to involve the people have aimed at showing the rest of the world that Tanzania is a democratic country in which the people are participating in their own governance. However, beneath these appearances, efforts to involve the people in the constitution-making process have been hollow. A clear example is the whole White Paper process. Here, the government prepared issues, which in its opinion were important for the country. Instead of letting the people discuss them, the government spelt out its own position and then asked the people to add any other comments provided those comments did not question the government's proposals. This of course fell far short of consulting or involving the people in the constitutional process.

Notes

1. See Nyerere, Julius K., 1973, *Freedom and Development*, Dar es Salaam: Oxford University Press, p. 70.

2. See Chidzero, Bernard T.G., 1961, *Tanganyika and International Trusteeship*, London: Oxford University Press.

3. See Read, James S.,1973, 'Bills of Rights in the Third World: Some Commonwealth Experiences,' Volume 6 *Verfassung und Recht in Ubersee*, p. 21; and Martin, Robert, 1974, *Personal Freedom and the Law in Tanzania: A Study of Socialist State Administration*, Nairobi: Oxford University Press, p. 38.

4. See Friedland, William H., *Vuta Kamba*, 1969, *The Development of the Trade Unions in Tanganyika*, Stanford, California: Stanford University and Hoover Institution Press.

5. See Naali, Shamshad, 'State Control over Co-operative Societies and Agricultural Marketing Boards,' in SHIVJI, Issa G. (ed.), *The State and the Working People in Tanzania*, London: CODESRIA, p. 132.

6. See Kapinga, Wilbert B.L., 1985, 'State Control of the Working Class Through Labour Legislation,' in SHIVJI, Issa G. (ed.), *The State and the Working People in Tanzania*, London: CODESRIA, p. 87.

7. Kasanga Tumbo was appointed Tanzanian High Commission to the Court of St James (Britain) and resigned after a short time.

8. See Pratt, Cranford, 1978, *The Critical Phase in Tanzania 1945-1968: Nyerere and the Emergence of a Socialist Strategy*, Nairobi: Oxford University Press, p. 123.

9. This was done under the Deportation Ordinance, 1921 (Chapter 38 of the Revised Laws of Tanzania).

10. See Said, Mohamed, 1994, 'Has the Present Tanzania Labour Movement Abdicated a Political Role?' Volume 2 Nos. 8 and 9 *Change*, August September, p. 50

11. See Mlimuka, A.K. and Kabudi, P.J., 1985, 'The State and the Party,' in Shivji, I.G. (ed.), *The State and the Working People in Tanzania*, Dakar, CODESRIA Book Series, p. 57 at 62.

12. See Msekwa, 1977, Pius, *Towards Party Supremacy*, Arusha: Eastern Africa Publications Limited, p. 22.

13. See Pratt, Cranford, 1974, *The Critical Phase in Tanzania 1945-1966: Nyerere and the Emergence of Socialist Strategy*, Cambridge: Cambridge University Press, p. 187.

14. See Government of The United Republic of Tanzania, 1968, *Report of the Presidential Commission on the Establishment of a Democratic One-Party State*, Dar es Salaam: Government Printer, p. 2 paragraph 8.

15. See Nyerere, Julius K., 1973, 'The Party Must Speak for the People.' In Nyerere, Julius K., *Freedom and Development*, Dar es Salaam: Oxford University Press, at pp. 30 and 32-33.

16. This was done through Act No. 8 of 1975 which declared that 'All political activities in Tanzania shall be conducted by or under the auspices of the Party.'

17. He is quoted in Hopkins, Raymond F., 1971, *Political Roles in a New State: Tanzania's First Decade*, New Haven and London: Yale University Press, p. 26.

18. See article 7 of the articles of the union. The articles of the Union and other relevant documents on the constitution are reproduced in Volume 3 of the Report of the Kisanga White Paper Committee.

19. This extension was done vide the Constituent Assembly Act, 1965 (Act No. 18 of 1965).

20. Other members of this Committee were Pius Msekwa, Asia Amour, Kanali Seif Bakari, Nicodemus Banduka, Hamisi Hemed, Jackson Kaaya, Rajabu Kheri, Peter Kisumo, Basheikh Mikidai, Beatrice Mhango, Hassan Nassor Moyo, Hamdan Muhidin, Daudi Mwakawago, Ngombale Mwiru, Ali Mzee, Abdallah Natepe, Juma Salum, Lawi Sijaona, na Peter Siyovelwa. See Government Notice No. 38 of 25 March 1977.

21. See Government Notice No. 39 of 25 March 1977.

22. See Shivji, Issa G., 1998, 'Problems of Constitution-making as a consensus-building: The Tanzanian Experience,' in Sichone, Owen (ed.), *The State and Constitutionalism*, Harare: Sapes Books, pp. 23 and 31.

23. See Chama Cha Mapinduzi, 1983, *NEC Proposals for Changes in the Constitution of the United Republic and the Constitution of the Revolutionary Government of Zanzibar*, Dodoma: C.C.M. Department of Propaganda and Mass Mobilisation.

24. Peter, Chris Maina, 1997, *Human Rights in Tanzania: Selected Cases and Materials*, Cologne: Rudiger Koppe Verlag.

25. This is the *Chama cha Kitaaluma cha Waalimu Tanzania* – an independent professional teachers' organisation.

26. See Tambila, Kapepwa I., 1995, 'The Transition to Multi-Party Democracy in Tanzania: From One State Party to Many State Parties,' *Verfassung and Richt in Ubresse* vol. 28 No. 4, p. 41.

27. The views of Tanganyika Law Society were recorded in the Commission's report. See Government of the United Republic of Tanzania, 1968, *Report of the Presidential Commission on the Establishment of a Democratic One Party State*, Dar es Salaam: Government Printer, Dar es Salaam.

28. Interestingly, after years in wilderness and notwithstanding his critical stance, lawyer Wolfgang Dourado is currently a Puisne Judge of the High Court of Zanzibar.

29. This was done through the Constitution (Fifth) (Amendment) Act, 1984 (Act No. 15 of 1984). On this see Lugakingira, K.S.K, 1991, 'Personal Liberty and Judicial Attitude: The Tanzanian Case,' Volume 17 *Eastern Africa Law Review*, 1990, p. 107; and Peter, Chris Maina, 1991, 'Five Years of Bill of Rights in Tanzania: Drawing a Balance Sheet,' Volume 18 *Eastern Africa Law Review*, p. 147.

30. See Tambila, Kapepwa I., 'The Transition to Multi-Party Democracy in Tanzania: From One State Party to Many State Parties,' op. cit.

31. See 'Team on Political Debate Formed,' *Sunday News* (Tanzania), 24 February 1991, p. 1. Also relevant are the following works: Tambila, Kapepwa I., 'The Transition to Multiparty Democracy in Tanzania: Some History and Missed Opportunities,' op. cit. p. 468; and Peter, Chris Maina, 1996, 'Determining the Pace of Change: The Law on Pluralism in Tanzania,' in Oloka-Onyango, Joseph *et al* (eds.), *Law and the Struggle for Democracy in East Africa*, Nairobi: Claripress, p. 511.

32. See 'One Year for Multi-Party Fact Finding,' *Daily News* (Tanzania), 28 February 1991.

33. The conference is well covered in SHIVJI, Issa G., 1998, 'Problems of Constitution-Making as Consensus-Building: The Tanzanian Experience,' in Sichone, Owen (ed.), *The State and Constitutionalism*, Harare: Sapes Books, p. 23 at p. 36.

34. The multiparty political system was adopted vide the Constitution (Eighth) (Amendment) Act, 1992 (Act No. 4 of 1992. This constitutional amendment was supplemented by the Political Parties Act, 1992 (Act No. 5 of 1992).

35. See Kimwaga, John, 1996, 'Tortuous Road to Multi-Partyism,' in *Family Mirror* (Tanzania) First Issue December, 1992. Also reproduced in Kibwana, Kivutha; Chris Maina Peter; and Joseph Oloka-Onyango (eds.), 1996, *In Search of Freedom and Prosperity: Constitutional Reform in East Africa*; Nairobi: Claripress, p. 55.

36. See the editorial entitled 'National Conference Needed Now,' in *Family Mirror* (Tanzania), First Issue December, 1993; and Juma, Ibrahim H., 1996, 'Constitution-Making in Tanzania: The Case for a National Conference,' in Oloka-Onyango, Joseph; Kivutha Kibwana and Chris Maina Peter (eds.), *The Law and the Struggle for Democracy in East Africa*, Nairobi: Claripress, p. 393.

37. The White Paper was Government Notice No. 1 of 1998.

38. The 13th amendment to the constitution of the United Republic of Tanzania was effected through Act No. 3 of 2000 entitled *Sheria za Mabadiliko ya Kumi na Tatu Katika Katiba ya Nchi*.

39. See Section 8 of Act No. 3 of 2000.

40. See Section 11 of Act No. 3 of 2000.

41. Ibid.

Bibliography

Bienefeld, M.A., 1979, 'Trade Unions, the Labour Process, and the Tanzanian State,' *Journal of Modern African Studies,* Volume 17. No.4

Bienen, Henry, 1967, 'The Ruling Party in the African One-Party State: TANU in Tanzania,' *Journal of Commonwealth Political Studies*, Volume 5.

Chidzero, Bernard T.G., 1961 *Tanganyika and International Trusteeship*, London: Oxford University Press.

Cole, J.S.R. and Denison, W.N., 1964, *Tanganyika: The Development of Its Laws and Constitution*, London: Stevens & Sons.

Coulson, Andrew (ed.), 1979, *African Socialism in Practice: The Tanzanian Experience*, Nottingham: Spokesman.

Coulson, Andrew, 1982, *Tanzania: A Political Economy*, Oxford: Clarendon Press.

Cranenburgh, Oda van, 1990, *The Widening Gyre: The Tanzania One-Party State and Policy Towards Rural Co-operatives*, Delft, The Netherlands: Eburon Publishers.

Fimbo, G. Mgongo, 1992, *Constitution Making and Courts in Tanzania*, Dar es Salaam: Faculty of Law.

Fortmann, Louise, 1980, *Peasants, Officials and Participation in Rural Tanzania: Experience with Villagisation and Decentralisation*, Ithaca, New York: Rural Development Committee of the Centre for International Studies of the Cornell University.

Freyhold, Michaela von, 1979, *Ujamaa Villages in Tanzania: Analysis of a Social Experiment*, London/ Ibadan and Nairobi: Heinemann Educational Books Ltd,.

Friedland, William H., 1969, *Vuta Kamba: The Development of Trade Unions in Tanganyika*, Stanford, California: Stanford University and Hoover Institution Press.

Government of the United Republic of Tanzania, 1968, *Report of the Presidential Commission on the Establishment of a Democratic One Party State*, Dar es Salaam: Government Printer, Dar es Salaam.

Government of the United Republic of Tanzania, 1992, *The Report and Recommendations of the Presidential Commission on Single Party or Multiparty System in Tanzania, 1991 on the Democratic System in Tanzania*, Dar es Salaam: Dar es Salaam University Press.

Havnevik, Kjell J., 1993, *Tanzania: The Limits to Development from Above*, Uppsala: The Scandinavian Institute of African Studies and Dar es Salaam: Mkuki na Nyota Publishers.

Hopkins, Raymond F., 1970, 'The Role of the M.P. in Tanzania,' *American Political Science Review*, Volume 64 No. 3.

Hopkins, Raymond F., 1971, *Political Roles in a New State: Tanzania's First Decade*, New Haven and London: Yale University Press.

Hyden, Goran, 1980, *Beyond Ujamaa in Tanzania: Underdevelopment and an Uncaptured Peasantry*, Berkeley and Los Angeles: University of California Press.

Kapinga, Wilbert B.L., 1985, 'State Control of the Working Class Through Labour Legislation,' in Shivji, Issa G. (ed.), *The State and the Working People in Tanzania*, London: CODESRIA.

Kibwana, Kivutha, Chris Maina Peter and Joseph Oloka-Onyango (eds.), 1996, *In Search of Freedom and Prosperity: Constitutional Reform in East Africa*, Nairobi: Claripress.

Kjekshus, Helge, 1974, 'Parliament in a One-Party State - The Bunge of Tanzania, 1965-70,' *Journal of Modern African Studies*, Volume 12 No. 1.

Legum, Colin and Geoffrey Mmari (eds.), 1995, *MWALIMU: The Influence of Nyerere*, London/ Dar es Salaam/ Trenton: James Currey/ Mkuki na Nyota and Africa World Press.

Listowel, Judith, 1965, *Making of Tanganyika*, London: Chatto and Windus.

Mapolu, Henry (ed.), 1976, *Workers and Management*, Dar es Salaam: Tanzania Publishing House, 1976.

Mapolu, Henry and Issa G. Shivji, 1984, *Vuguvugu la Wafanyakazi Nchini Tanzania*, Kampala: East Africa URM Contact Group.

Martin, Robert, 1976, *Personal Freedom in Tanzania: A Study of Socialist State Administration*, Nairobi: Oxford University Press.

Mihyo, Paschal B., 1983, *Industrial Conflict and Change in Tanzania*, Dar es Salaam: Tanzania Publishing House.

Mohiddin, Ahmed, 1981, *African Socialism in Two Countries*, London and Totowa, New Jersey: Croom Helm and Barnes & Noble Books.

Msekwa, Pius, 1995, *The Transition to Multiparty Democracy*, Dar es Salaam: Tema Publishers Company Ltd and Tanzania Publishing House.

Msekwa, Pius, 1977, *Towards Party Supremacy*, Arusha: Eastern Africa Publications Ltd.

Mtaki, Cornel K. and Michael Okema (eds.), 1994, *Constitutional Reforms and Democratic Governance in Tanzania*, Dar es Salaam: Friedrich Naumann Stiftung.

Mukurasi, L., 1991, *Post Abolished: One Woman's Struggle for Employment Rights in Tanzania*, London: The Women's Press.

Mvungi, Sengondo E.A., 1991, *Constitutionalism and the Status of the Legislature in a One Party System: The Case of Tanzania*, LL.M Thesis, University of Hamburg, Federal Republic of Germany.

Mvungi, Sengondo E.A., 1986, *Impact of Party Supremacy Doctrine on the Democratic Process of Government in Tanzania: A Constitutional and Administrative Law Perspective*, LL.M Dissertation, Faculty of Law, University of Dar es Salaam.

Mwalusanya, James L., 1994, 'Conditions for Functioning of a Democratic Constitution,' in Mtaki, Cornel K. and Michael Okema (eds.), *Constitutional Reforms and Governance in Tanzania*, Dar es Salaam: Friedrich Naumann Stiftung.

Mwapachu, Juma Volter, 1979, 'Operation Planned Villages in Rural Tanzania: A Revolutionary Strategy for Development,' in COULSON, Andrew (ed.), *African Socialism in Practice: The Tanzanian Experience*, Nottingham: Spokesman.

Mwansasu, Bismarck and Cranford Pratt (eds.), 1979, *Towards Socialism in Tanzania*, Dar es Salaam: Tanzania Publishing House.

Nyalali, Francis L., 1975, *Aspects of Industrial Conflict: A Case Study of Trade Disputes in Tanzania 1967-1973*, Nairobi: East Africa Literature Bureau.

Nyerere, Julius K., 1966, *Freedom and Unity*, Dar es Salaam: Oxford University Press.

Nyerere, Julius K., 1967, *Freedom and Development*, Dar es Salaam: Oxford University Press.

Nyerere, Julius K., 1968, *Freedom and Socialism*, Dar es Salaam: Oxford University Press.

Okema, Michael and Jwani T. Mwaikusa (eds.), 1992, *Constitutions and Opposition in Africa*, Dar es Salaam: Friedrich Ebert Stiftung.

Oloka-Onyango, Kivutha Kibwana and Chris Maina Peter (eds.), 1996, *The Law and the Struggle for Democracy in East Africa*, Nairobi: Claripress.

O'neill, Norman and Kemal Mustafa (eds.), 1990, *Capitalism, Socialism and the Development Crisis in Tanzania*, Aldershot, Avebury: Gower Publishing Company.

Peter, Chris Maina, 1996, 'Determining the Pace of Change: The Law on Pluralism in Tanzania,' in Oloka-Onyango, Joseph et all (eds.), *Law and the Struggle for Democracy in East Africa*, Nairobi: Claripress.

Peter, Chris Maina, 1997, *Human Rights in Tanzania: Selected Cases and Materials*, Cologne: Rudiger Koppe Verlag.

Pratt, Cranford, 1976, *The Critical Phase in Tanzania 1945-1968: Nyerere and the Emergence of a Socialist Strategy*, Cambridge: Cambridge University Press.

Rabl, Kurt, 1967, 'Constitutional Development and the Law of the United Republic of Tanzania: An Outline,' *Jahrbuch des Öffentlichen Rechts der Gegenwart*, Volume 16.

Resnick, Idrian N., 1981, *The Long Transition: Building Socialism in Tanzania*, New York and London: Monthly Review Press.

Seaton, Earl E. and Kirilo Japhet, 1967, *The Meru Land Case*, Nairobi: East African Publishing House.

Seaton, Earl E. and Joseph S. Warioba, 1978, 'The Constitution of Tanzania: An Overview,' *Eastern Africa Law Review,* Volumes 11-14.

Shivji, Issa G., 1995, 'The Role of Law and Ujamaa in the Ideological Formation of Tanzania,' *Social & Legal Studies,* Volume 4.

Shivji, Issa G., 1978, 'The State of the Constitution and the Constitution of the State in Tanzania', *Eastern Africa Law Review,* Volumes 11-14.

ShivjI, Issa G. (ed.), 1985, *The State and the Working People in Tanzania,* London: CODESRIA.

Shivji, Issa G., 1986, *Law, State and the Working Class in Tanzania,* London: James Currey.

Shivji, Issa G., 1998, 'Problems of Constitution-Making as Consensus-Building: The Tanzanian Experience,' in Sichone, Owen (ed.), *The State and Constitutionalism,* Harare: Sapes Books.

Srivastava, B.P., 1978-1981, *The Constitution of the United Republic of Tanzania 1977 - Some Salient Features - Some Riddles,* Dar es Salaam: Dar es Salaam University Press, 1983. (See also *Eastern Africa Law Review,* Volumes 11-14.

Swantz, Marja L., 1985, *Women in Development: A Creative Role Denied? The Case of Tanzania,* London: Hurst.

Tambila, Kapepwa I., 1995, 'The Transition to Multiparty Democracy in Tanzania: Some History and Missed Opportunities,' *Verfassung und Recht in Übersee,* Volume 28 No. 4.

Tenga, Nakazael and Chris Maina Peter, 1996, 'The Right to Organise as Mother of All Rights: The Experience of Women Organisations in Tanzania,' *Journal of Modern African Studies,* Volume 34 No. 1.

Tordoff, William, 1965, 'Parliament in Tanzania,' *Journal of Commonwealth Political Studies,* Volume 3.

Tordoff, William and Ali A. Mazrui, 1972, 'The Left and the Super-Left in Tanzania,' *Journal of Modern African Studies,* Volume 10, No. 3.

Tripp, Aili Mari, 1992, 'Local Organisations, Participation, and the State in Urban Tanzania,' in Hyden, Goran and Michael Bratton (eds.), *Governance and Politics in Africa,* Boulder & London: Lynne Rienner Publishers.

Vuorela, Ulla, 1987, *The Women's Question and the Modes of Human Reproduction: An Analysis of a Tanzanian Village,* Helsinki: The Finish Society for Development Studies and Finish Anthropological Society.

WELCH, Claude E., Jr., 1978, 'The Right of Association in Ghana and Tanzania,' *Journal of Modern African Studies,* Volume 16 No. 4 .

Westerlund, David, 1982, 'Freedom of Religion under Socialist Rule in Tanzania - 1961-1977,' *Journal of Church and State,* Volume 24 No. 1.

Williams, David V., 1982, 'State Coercion Against Peasant Farmers: The Tanzania Case,' *Journal of Legal Pluralism,* Volume 20.

Mixed Results in Uganda's Constitutional Development: An Assessment

Nyangabyaki Bazaara

The 1995 Constitution represents a fairly radical reconstitution of the organs of the state. Certainly Uganda has not had a constitution that has attempted to effect radical change in the organs of the state and their relationship with the people. There are many things [in the constitution] that point in a new direction... In spite of the radical changes, [however,] there are severe limitations in the rights of association, in political expression and opposition.[1]

Introduction

Both the supporters and critics of the 1995 constitution are united in agreement that, despite its shortcomings, it was a fairly radical departure from all previous constitutions.[2] The 1995 constitution is different in as far as it was crafted through a protracted process involving a significant number of Ugandans and also in as far as it contains new constitutional innovations.[3] Against this background the 1995 constitution ought to be a durable foundation for constitutionalism in Uganda. However, the question remains: will the 1995 constitution work where the previous ones failed? After all, African constitutional experience reveals that elites have been manipulating constitutions to entrench themselves in power since independence.[4] In addition, and as Mahmood Mamdani argues, 'the terrain of constitutionalism has never been and cannot be an uncontested one.'[5] Whether or not a given constitution can become a basis for constitutionalism is not predetermined. Therefore, whether or not the culture of constitutionalism is growing as a result of the 1995 constitution is a pertinent question for students of constitutional development in Uganda.[6]

The objective of this paper is to examine constitutional issues that emerged in 1999 and make a critical analysis as to whether or not there is a discernible march towards constitutionalism. The paper is divided into 3 parts. Section one provides the historical context within which the new constitution was crafted. Section two highlights issues that emerged in 1999 to show the flaws or progress in the process of constitutionalism. Section three concludes the paper.

A violent history of political change and the necessity of a new constitution

The 1962 constitutional framework within which Uganda regained independence proved to be undurable. Within a space of less than five years, it was replaced by the 1966 interim constitution which in turn gave way to the 1967 constitution. Major provisions of the 1967 constitution were also thrown out by the military after the coup of 1971. Thereafter, the period 1971-1986 was characterised by unbridled dictatorship. In order to appreciate the implications of this onslaught on constitutionalism, we need to examine the manner in which constitutional amendments were introduced, the kinds of powers that were affected, and how these changes affected the operation of state structures as well as civil and political liberties.

The 1962 independence constitution was based on a compromise of various political interests. The Uganda Peoples Congress (UPC) formed an alliance with *Kabaka Yekka* (KY) to win state power from the Democratic Party (DP). Yet the interests that had coalesced under those two parties were opposed to each other. KY was a party of monarchists whose ultimate ambition was to safeguard the interests of Buganda inside or outside the Ugandan framework. In contrast, the UPC, a party of peasants, workers, some traders and intellectuals was avowedly nationalist. In the event, since the Buganda monarchists could not secure a separate existence from Uganda, they successfully negotiated a federal arrangement for Buganda which was entrenched in the 1962 constitution. Under this arrangement, Buganda retained powers over the local police, primary education, local forests, etc. In addition, the Baganda neo-traditionalists successfully blocked the advance of democratisation in local government under the independence constitution. Buganda's members to the national parliament were to be indirectly elected.

When Uganda attained independence, executive powers were vested in the office of the prime minister. When the posts of president and vice president were introduced in 1963, Kabaka Edward Mutesa became the first president and William Nadiope, the Kyabazinga of Busoga, became the vice president. However, the posts of president and vice president were more or less ceremonial. Executive powers were in the hands of the Prime Minister Milton Obote.

From about 1964, differences between the Buganda monarchists and the UPC began to surface. The touchstone was the issue of a referendum which, under the 1962 independence constitution, had to be held within two years after independence to resolve the problem of the 'lost counties'.

The 'lost counties' were disputed areas between the kingdoms of Bunyoro-Kitara and Buganda ever since the imposition of colonial rule when Bunyoro lost those areas to Buganda.

While Prime Minister Milton Obote was determined to follow through this constitutional provision, i.e holding a referendum in which the inhabitants of the 'lost counties' would vote either to remain in Buganda, become independent of both Buganda and Bunyoro or return to Bunyoro, Kabaka Mutesa and the Mengo government tried to block or manipulate the referendum. For example, Mutesa tried to rig the referendum by settling ex-service men in the disputed counties. He also shot down 9 Banyoro peasants gathered in a market place to show off his power and intimidate the voters. The 1964 referendum in which the voters in Buyaga and Bugangaizi chose to return to Bunyoro marked the beginning of confrontation between Mengo and the central government that culminated in the 1966 crisis entailing the abrogation of the independence constitution and the battle of Mengo. The unrest that followed in Buganda was clamped down with military might and a state of emergency declared over Buganda until 1971.

Before the battle of Mengo, the UPC government had introduced the 1966 interim constitution. The manner of its introduction was extremely controversial. First, the 1966 interim constitution was introduced without any discussion. As Abu Mayanja remarked during a parliamentary session, ' I know that the new constitution was dropped in our pigeonholes, we read it after we left parliament and after we had been sworn in'.[7] This meant that many people did not respect the 'pigeon hole' constitution and as such it could not become a basis of constitutionalism in Uganda.

Secondly, the executive usurped the powers of parliament. For example, during the debate on the Administrations (Kingdom) Bill, 1966, it was discovered that not only were the powers of local administrations being transferred to the district commissioners but also government was trying to usurp powers to make laws from parliament. Section 24 of the Administrations (Western Kingdoms and Busoga) Act empowered government to make laws, subject to the constitution, (a) in respect to any matter for which it was required or permitted to make laws, (b) public security and (c) functions it was required or permitted to carry out. Abu Mayanja quipped:

> Now this obviously escaped us during the previous time, but here we
> have an opportunity to correct it, because it is preposterous, Mr.
> Speaker, for us to speak of Government making laws...In other words,
> Section 24 is conferring power to make laws upon Government that is

to say upon the Ruler and his Council of Ministers, whereas according to the constitution, and indeed according to common sense, the power to make laws should be vested in the Legislature...

During the same period, the executive diminished the power of the judiciary. For example, the court cases that were brought against the government, such as those revolving around the arrest of five ministers and members of the Lukiiko who called the central government remove its capital from Kampala revealed that the judiciary was too weak to contain the executive.

Take the case of the five arrested ministers. The Obote government had deported them to Karamoja. Grace Ibingira, one of the ex-ministers, applied for a writ of *habeas corpus* to the high court arguing that, under the 1962 constitution, it was unconstitutional for government to deport its own citizens. When the court ordered the release of the ministers, the Obote government transported them to Entebbe, where they were rearrested under emergency regulations in Buganda. In addition, the Obote government also forced parliament to pass a Deportation (Validation) Act, which retroactively from 27 July 1966, sought to indemnify government from all penalties and liabilities arising out of deportation orders that had been served to the five ministers. In response, Ibingira challenged the validity of the Deportation (Validation) Act as being unconstitutional. The judges of the High Court held that the Act as well as the 1966 interim constitution were unconstitutional. However, Godfrey Binaisa, the attorney-general, challenged the judges arguing that since none had been sworn in as judges under the 1966 interim constitution; they could not turn around and declare that constitution invalid. Ibingira appealed to the East African Court of Appeal which simply upheld the government side!

The powers of the judiciary *vis-à-vis* the executive were put to further test in respect to the arrest of Matovu who was, before the crisis, a county chief and a member of the Lukiiko (the Buganda local parliament). After the battle for Mengo, Matovu and others were arrested on the ground that they had participated in the controversial resolution of the Buganda Lukiiko calling on the central government remove its capital from Buganda soil. The bid to get Matovu released raised issues about the legitimacy of the 1966 interim constitution. The Buganda chiefs filed a civil suit No. 206 of 1966 seeking the High Court of Uganda to declare that the assumption of all powers by Prime Minister Obote was a violation of the 1962 constitution and that Kabaka Mutesa was still the president. The High Court, however, appears to have been too scared to declare that the interim constitution was invalid.

The trend towards concentrating power in the executive and whittling down the importance of the legislature and the judiciary was further revealed in the government proposals that became the 1967 constitution. First, the president was put beyond legal scrutiny. Article 24 (3) of the 1967 constitution stated that the president 'shall not be liable to any proceedings whatsoever in any court'.[8] Whereas the 1962 constitution shielded the director of public prosecutions from control of the executive and political manipulation, the 1967 constitution squarely put the DPP under the control of the attorney general. In addition, the executive could appoint and dismiss public servants including cabinet members without checks from other organs.

A.A. Nekyon argued persuasively,

> Turning to civil liberties, our rights could be suspended summarily under the proposals and there was no recourse to the courts to find out why they had been suspended. This was the biggest indication of autocracy. The members were giving the President power to appoint everybody, dismiss everybody, nominate one third of the parliament and detain them in the bargain...The concentration of powers in one person was not justified. Some of the powers given to the President were excessive. There should be a balance between the office of the President and the Judiciary, and the system of Parliament.[9]

In effect the bill of rights was also transformed; restrictions were put on the enjoyment of those rights.[10]

The 1971 coup sealed what was already an established fact: the predominance of the executive power. The coup makers did not lose time; they abolished rights to organise in political parties and parliament. Hence, the power of making laws was taken over by the executive; the president was empowered to make laws by decree. The judiciary was cowed into silence. Not only was the chief justice, Ben Kiwanuka, killed but also the everyday operation of the judiciary was interfered with. As Oloka-Onyango has argued, this trend

> meant that the constitution was no longer "supreme law"; that it could be altered without reference to parliament, and finally that Parliament lost its law-making powers to the head of State - now empowered to rule by Presidential decree. In effect this made the President not only the "supreme law" of the land, but also the sole law-maker.[11]

It took the intervention of the Tanzania Peoples Defence Forces to oust Amin from power in 1979. Although the overthrow of Amin by a combined force of exiles and the Tanzanian army was called liberation from violence and dictatorship, subsequent events proved the opposite. Even the supposedly civilian Obote II government, a government that ascended to power through ballot box, abused the rights of its citizens and many innocent people were victims of extra-judicial killings.

In summary, prior to the commencement of the process that culminated in the promulgation of the new constitution in 1995, it is clear that politicians recrafted constitutions to buttress themselves in power. Given that the amendments were not based on popular discussion and compromise, many Ugandans did not respect the pre-1995 constitutions. This had disastrous consequences for the culture of constitutionalism. In Uganda, political change has been extremely violent and unconstitutional. In a situation where the executive was not subjected to checks and balances, the relationship between state organs and the people was characterised by dictatorship and disrespect of human rights. The people of Uganda lost close relatives and friends because of state-inspired violence. It was with relief that when the NRM came to power, it tried to curb state-inspired violence and to reintroduce some semblance of rule of law, although the right of people to organise in political parties continued to be curtailed. Most important was the NRM's decision to make a new constitution. It was envisaged that the new constitution would enjoy popular respect and legitimacy and henceforth all political change would be constitutional and peaceful. In order to ensure respect and legitimacy for the new constitutional dispensation, it was decided that the people should fully participate in the making of the new constitution.

The Constitutional Commission and the Constituent Assembly

The process of making a new constitution began in 1988 with the appointment of a Constitutional Commission, which produced a draft constitution in December 1992. This was followed by the election of the Constituent Assembly in 1994, which debated the draft constitution and produced a new constitution that was promulgated in October 1995.[12]

The appointment of the members of the commission was very controversial and probably affected the kind of constitution that eventually emerged. Critics have argued that the biggest drawback was that the members of the Constitutional Commission were handpicked and many were deemed to be sympathetic to the NRM. Organised political interests such as political parties were not invited to send their own chosen representatives. Questions have been raised about the manner in which the Constitutional Commission went about 'educating' people. It has been argued that the kind of questions that the commission posed and the debates it organised were designed in such a way as to favour the NRM as against the multi-partyists. Most controversial was the Constitutional Commission's suggestion that political party activities be frozen until some future date. In short, the Constitutional Commission created a framework for the Constituent Assembly to proscribe freedom of assembly and association.

The decision to elect a Constituent Assembly was no doubt a movement forward in the history of constitutional-making in Uganda. Although the 1967 constitution was a product of debate and discussion, the problem was that it was passed by a parliament whose prescribed time had long expired. Parliament was operating unconstitutionally. In addition, the choice of a protracted and time-consuming process was also new and commendable, for this approach was the only way to generate the much needed consensus that would make the new constitution respected and obeyed by all.[13] For that, commentators have argued that it was truly a serious attempt to make constitutionalism a reality.

However, there were flaws in the the way the CA was constituted. Those individuals who came through the electoral process were elected on 'individual' merit rather than on the basis of organisational support. This meant that they could be influenced to support wrong motions if they were promised state patronage. Indeed, many of the debates in the CA were coloured by political calculations of accessing state patronage or being elected as parliamentarians in the post-CA political order. This was particularly so because the law did not forbid CA delegates from standing for parliamentary elections after the promulgation of the new constitution.

It has also been argued that NRM supporters were determined to support the NRM line whether it was right or wrong rather than to debate constitutional issues on their own merits. There are instances when useful motions were not supported simply because they had been moved by self-confessed multi-partyists.[14] In the process, the CA recommended that the NRM 'system' should continue for another five years, with political party activities proscribed and that a decision as to whether or not the 'Movement system' should be replaced by a multi-party system would be decided by a referendum four years after the 1996 presidential and parliamentary elections. The controversial article 269 banning political activities remains one of the clauses in the 1995 constitution that contradicts the otherwise excellent bill of rights section and dilutes the protracted, time consuming and sometimes painful efforts put into the constitution-making process. No doubt, this article is one of the biggest drawbacks to the growth of constitutionalism in present-day Uganda.

It should be noted that the constitution contains some new innovations. First, the language is gender–sensitive. Secondly, there are elaborate provisions to advance the rights of women, the disabled and children. In addition, the constitution provides for the rights to organise for categories of workers such as medical workers, rights that had been denied by previous constitutions.

What then is the progress after the promulgation of the constitution? Is there progress towards durable constitutionalism? In the following section we highlight those issues that emerged in 1999 and assess whether or not a culture of constitutionalism is growing in Uganda.

Constitutional issues in 1999

Armed insurgency in northern and western Uganda

One of the assumptions behind the making of the 1995 constitution was that this would usher in an era of peace and the peaceful resolution of conflict. Peace is an important ingredient for constitutionalism. However, even with the new constitution, the resort to armed methods to address political issues still prevails. The Lord's Resistance Army (LRA) has continued to maraud the north for close to a decade and the Allied Democratic Forces (ADF) has destabilised the western region of the country.

One aspect of the armed insurgency in northern and western Uganda is the involvement of neighbouring countries. In the year under review, Sudan continued to provide armed support to the LRA and ADF. The success of foreign forces in destabilising Uganda may partly be related to the fact that there is a missing link in Uganda's democratisation process. Disenchanted people resort to foreign support to force the system to respond to their demands.[15] But most important the culture of constitutionalism can only grow if Uganda has peaceful relations with its neigbours and internally the democratic process accommodates people of diverse opinions.

During 1999, there was an attempt to use peaceful means to end the conflict in northern and western Uganda. An Amnesty Bill was passed in December 1999 to establish a 'legal framework within which the government can implement its policy of reconciliation and facilitate its efforts to eliminate rebel elements in some parts of the country.'[16] Since it was passed in December 1999, its practical achievements can only be realised in the year 2000, which is outside of scope of this assessment. However, the point here is that the deepening of a culture of constitutionalism requires that Ugandans develop a culture of democracy and also nurture peaceful relations with its neighbours. Yet the persistence of armed insurgency is testimony to the fact that there are still gaps in the culture of constitutionalism and the democratisation process. Some observers are inclined to think that the 1995 constitution has not provided an acceptable legal way to express dissent. As a result, people have been resorting to arms in order to express their dissatisfaction with the NRM government. The ban on political party activities has closed avenues for those who do not believe in the 'Movement systems. Article 269 of the 1995 constitution prohibits political parties from:

a)   opening and operating branches;

b)   holding delegates conferences;

c)   holding public rallies;

d)   sponsoring or offering platform to or in any way campaigning for or against a candidate for any public elections; and

e)   carrying on any activities that may interfere with the Movement political system for the time being in force.[17]

This article contradicts two fundamental rights – the right to associate and the right to dissent. Article 29 clause (e) states that every person shall have the right to 'freedom of association, which shall include the freedom to form and join associations or unions, including trade unions and *political* and other civic organisations'(emphasis added).[18] Second, those who believe in multi-partyism have tried to defy the provisions of article 269. In the past, elections under the Movement system have been aligned along party interests and multi-partyists have continued to meet and *politick* sometimes in disguised form. It is not a surprise that the activities of the Foundation for African Development (FAD) are always a target of the state. FAD is generally believed to be a cloak behind which the Democratic Party hides although it is registered as an NGO. In 1999, state officials broke up two seminars organised by FAD. One seminar for civic education in Moyo was prevented from taking place in January 1999. The seminar was

> broken up for political reasons. A local FAD organizer informed the organization's officials that the district council chairperson had described the FAD seminar as a multiparty meeting intended to cause disruption in the district, and that the meeting should be prevented from taking place.[19]

In another incident in Mpigi, an official of FAD was harassed in April 1999. Once again it was believed that the seminar was a multiparty function.[20] What is interesting to note is the fact that the state in some instances uses extra-constitutional or extra-legal actions against political parties. Seminars, for example, are not part of the list of activities prohibited by article 269.

Even more important for the culture of constitutionalism are the accusations against the Movement system of being 'undemocratic, corrupt and opportunistic'. Col. Kiiza Besigye wrote a statement that was widely publicised in the media. He was accused of having used a wrong forum to air his grievances.[21] However, Kiiza Besigye's criticisms point to the fact that unless the NRM can itself practice internal democracy, its moral claim that political parties are up to no good will remain hollow.

Uganda's involvement in the Congo
Another thorny constitutional issue in 1999 was the continued presence of Ugandan troops in the Congo. In a speech to parliament in 1998, President Yoweri Kaguta Museveni argued that:

> Our involvement in Congo (indirectly last year and a bit more directly this year) is mainly because of the threats to our security that emanate from there in the form of NALU in the past and, more recently, ADF...Therefore, Mr. Speaker, may I restate our position. We are in Congo primarily for our own security.[22]

Although, it is perfectly in order for a country to ensure its security interests, the constitutional snag is that the president (executive) did not seek the approval of parliament as stipulated in the Ugandan constitution. According to article 210 (d) parliament shall make laws regulating the Uganda Peoples Defence Forces (UPDF), and in particular for the 'deployment of troops outside Uganda.'[23] The continued presence of the UPDF in Congo remains a very controversial aspect as far as constitutionalism is concerned.

The functioning of state organs
Parliament
Parliament improved its performance by censuring Sam Kutesa, the minister for Finance in charge of planning and investment. One hundred and sixteen members of parliament signed a petition of censure. A motion was moved citing

> Kutesa's ministerial portfolio and being a chairman of the Entebbe cargo handling firm, ENHAS, as constituting a conflict of interest, contrary to the leadership code of conduct. Kutesa was also accused of causing financial loss to Uganda Airlines by allowing ENHAS to buy the national carrier's shares in the cargo firm below market value and also writing off as a bad debt US $ 400,000.[24]

Members of parliament numbering 152 voted to censure the minister who was dropped in the subsequent cabinet reshuffle. Kutesa was the second minister after Jim Muhwezi who was censured in 1998. Shortly after, parliament sought to censure the vice president, Specioza Wandira Kazibwe, and the two ministers of state in Agriculture, Lawrence Kezimbira Miyingo and Kibirige Ssebunnya. It was believed that the shs. 3.4 billion meant for the construction of valley dams in Masaka, Mbarara and Luwero districts was utilised inappropriately.[25] To save the vice president, the president dropped her from the Ministry of Agriculture. We need to note here that parliament played a positive role in 1999 by acting as a check on the executive arm of government. This has enhanced the culture of constitutionalism.

The relationship between the Executive and Parliament
Despite these positive developments in the functioning of parliament, it still remained overshadowed by the executive. Mention has already been made regarding how the executive deployed troops in Congo without recourse to parliament. In addition, there were some instances in which the executive tried to bulldoze parliament to pass legislation, particularly those laws aimed at attracting foreign investors or when the executive was under pressure from foreign donors.

One of the issues around which the executive and parliament clashed was the legislation to liberalise the production of electricity. Until 1999 the production and distribution of electricity was monopolised by the Uganda Electricity Board. To allow other private investors to enter the business of producing and distributing electricity required a new law. The executive wanted parliament to expeditiously pass a law liberalising the production of electricity so that foreign investors could embark on the construction of dams at Bujagali and Karuma falls. However, the environmental consequences related to dam construction at these sites had not been assessed and, therefore, parliament insisted that such an assessment be made first, much to the displeasure of the executive. During a World Bank-sponsored workshop in Kampala, President Museveni accused MPs of delaying the process. He argued that this could cause a 'political crisis'.[26]

> These days I am very disgruntled, I am tired and sick of wiseacres, everybody is an authority and they do not listen to my advice. There is a lot of wastage of time...Parliament is another confusion. Traditionally, I have been having bureaucrats but now there are MPs and sometimes the World Bank comes from the other side. How many wars shall I fight?...World Bank told me Uganda was in danger of too much electricity. We have struck a compromise with Mr. Adams that we can have a dam at Bujagali and then Karuma afterwards, but still I have a problem with parliament.[27]

In response to this attack by the executive, members of parliament passed a resolution that parliamentarians 'have no intention, have never had intentions and will never have an intention to cause a crisis'.[28] Major Okwiri Rabwoni (Youth MP Western) argued that the youth 'look on with trepidation when the process of democratisation and constitutionalism is about to be halted'. Elly Karuhanga, speaking on behalf of parliamentary committees, argued that it was the executive and not parliament that was to blame.[29] The most important thing about this exchange between the executive and parliament is that it sensitised the public about the self-assertion of the parliament vis-a-vis the executive. In a sense, this exchange could have enhanced the culture of constitutionalism. This is readily discernible in the letters that appeared in the media. For example, Peter Nyanzi wrote:

> Parliament has shown that even a poor and needy country like Uganda reserves the right to study investment proposals, take them through a sifting process and negotiate for what is best for its people and on the best terms possible. However long it takes, however good the investment projects are, even in a poor country, they should be in line with established regulations and prescribed procedure. It is amazing and ironical that even in the light of the hastily made shoddy deals with companies like Midroc, Westmont and Tahar Fourati's Africa Continental Hotels, the Government is now criticizing parliament for 'delaying' to approve the AES power deal.[30]

It would appear that although the executive is able to assert itself, it also has to contend with parliament and outside forces. In this case we are not only referring to the World Bank, IMF and other donor conditionalities but also the forces of globalisation in general. As the president indicated, sometimes he is under pressure to create an enabling environment for foreign investors. This pressure forces the executive to compel parliament to pass certain laws without thorough debate. Such pressure from donors or investors can be detrimental to the maintenance of adequate checks and balances between the executive and parliament and, therefore, to the culture of constitutionalism. It should be recalled that in the history of constitutions, the first casualty of the internal conflicts or outside pressure is parliament. For a country whose constitutional development is still fragile, the danger of the executive usurping the role of parliament is ever present and can only be averted when there are organised political forces in the country committed to the culture of constitutionalism.

Drawbacks in Parliament

Although parliament carried out a lot of anti-corruption activities, it had a number of weaknesses. The weaknesses of parliament after the promulgation of the constitution were as follows. Even though it had asserted independence from the executive by, for example, censuring Ministers Kirunda Kevejinja, Jim Muhwezi and Sam Kutesa over corruption and conflict of interest, it has failed to exert its influence on issues such as troops deployment and fiscal matters. Indeed, the executive continues to dole out patronage to favourites through cabinet posts. Is it surprising that parliament approved the expansion of cabinet? Recognising the dangers involved, Onapito Ekolomoit, the MP for Amuria county, introduced a motion intended to enhance the separation of powers between different organs of the state. His motion targeted article 113 of the 1995 constitution which provides that 'cabinet members shall be appointed by the President with the approval of parliament from among members of parliament or persons qualified to be elected members of parliament'.[31]

The Onapito motion proposed that once a parliamentarian is appointed cabinet minister, that individual should automatically be dropped from parliament. In support of the motion, Mugisha Muntu argued that the bill would 'advance democratic practice, improve efficiency in government, enhance transparency and undermine opportunism and intrigue'.[32] Unfortunately, the motion was rejected by parliament.

The reduction of the number of cabinet posts and the privatisation of public enterprises has reduced the resources at the disposal of the executive to dispense patronage. However, this has not significantly improved the operation of parliament. The executive can still take initiatives aimed at co-opting a particular vocal individual. As Oloka-Onyango argued:

> The Legislature remains trapped by the one phenomenon that has dogged movement politics from the outset, the factor of "individual" merit. Given this factor, it is questionable that parliament (as a group) can do little more than nibble at the edifice of state power and control. Since each member is in the house as an individual, they are so easily divided on the basis of *individual* interest and concerns. Of particular concern is the pavlovian dangling of cabinet posts in order to secure compliance on an issue in which the executive has staked out a particular interest. This explains why parliament as a body can demand the resignation of a single individual (even if he /she is a powerful one like Muhwezi) and not demand that the whole government resigns.[33]

Given the massive dependence of Uganda on foreign funds, the sovereignty of the country is compromised. To a considerable extent the legislature has not been at the forefront to debate what kind of economic policies to adopt or rejected. As is well known, IMF/World Bank-sponsored programmes are conditionalities for Uganda's continued access to foreign loans and grants. Quite often the donors through the executive have had their way, thereby transforming the legislature from the supreme organ in the land into a mere rubber stamp of policies dictated from abroad. A case in point is the budgeting process. It is well known that donors overshadow the entire process. Before a budget is passed on to parliament it has to be reviewed by donors, including the IMF and the World Bank. Constitutionalism culture is thus undermined because parliament—which is supposed to debate budgets—is reduced to a rubber stamp.

Another crucial issue is whether parliament respects constitutional rules when conducting its own business. The litmus test for parliament's credibility was when it passed the Referendum and other Provisions Act apparently without the requisite quorum.[34] Speaker Francis Ayume claimed that there was a quorum, not on the basis of the physical count of the MPs in the house but on the basis of those who had signed in the register. This became extremely controversial.

In September 1999, Paul Ssemwogerere and Zachary Olum petitioned the constitutional court. They prayed the court to declare the Referendum and Other Provisions Act null and void. They argued that the Act was not valid for two reasons. First, it was enacted without a quorum in parliament. Second, that it was enacted after the expiry of the date stipulated in the constitution. The petition was thrown out on the technical ground that the petitioners could not use parliamentary records as evidence without the permission of the speaker, among other things.

There are two constitutional issues here. First, is the problem of not respecting the constitutional provisions, i.e., enacting the Act after the date stipulated in the constitution had long passed. The second, is the operation of the parliament without a quorum. Article 88 of the 1995 constitution stipulates that 'the quorum of Parliament shall be one-third of all members of parliament'. Article 89 (1) stipulates that 'except as otherwise prescribed by this constitution or any law consistent with this Constitution, any question proposed for decision of Parliament shall be determined by a majority of votes of the members present and voting'.[35] Since the Act was passed without a quorum consisting of physically present members, it is arguable that the Referendum Act was passed unconstitutionally. Given that some of the parliamentarians boycotted the proceedings, this undermines the progress towards constitutionalism.

The constitution empowers parliament to enact a number of laws within a given time frame. Article 41 (1) of the constitution provides that 'every citizen has a right of access to information in the possession of the State or any other organ or agency of State except where the release of the information is likely to prejudice the security or sovereignty of the State or interference with the right to the privacy of any other person'. Clause 2 provides that 'Parliament shall make laws prescribing the classes of information referred to in clause (1) of this article and the procedure for obtaining access to that information'.

The constitution further provides in article 32 (1) 'Notwithstanding anything in this constitution, the State shall take affirmative action in favour of groups marginalized on the basis of gender, age, disability or any other reason created by history, tradition or custom, or the purpose of redressing imbalances which exist against them'. Clause 2 provides that 'Parliament shall make relevant laws, including laws for the establishment of an equal opportunities commission, for the purpose of giving full effect to clause (1) of this article'.

In article 270 parliament was required to make 'laws relating to the registration of political parties and organisations'. Under article 125, parliament is supposed to establish a National Planning Authority and prescribe its duties and functions. Article 244 provides that parliament shall make laws regarding the exploitation of minerals, the sharing of royalties arising from mineral exploitation, etc. None of these laws were enacted by the end of 1999. This failure of parliament to carry out such constitutional mandates undermines the progress made so far in the direction of constitutionalism.

The Judiciary and the Executive

The relationship between the judiciary and the executive remained strained in the year under review. In the history of Uganda, there has been little independence of the judiciary from the executive. According to article 126, among the principles that guide the courts of law is that 'justice shall not be delayed'. Under article 128 (1), the courts are supposed to be 'independent and shall not be subject to the control or direction of any person or authority'. Clause (2) stipulates that 'no person or authority shall interfere with the courts or judicial officers in the exercise of their judicial functions'.[36] In practice court cases are delayed and courts are rarely independent of the executive.

One of the mechanisms used by the executive to erode the judiciary's independence is the executive's control of finances and general decisions regarding the welfare of the officers in the judiciary. As Justice J.H. Ntabgoba noted:

> Even if we took the expression "interfere" by its direct meaning we are not short of those individuals or authorities that interfere with our magistrates in the exercise of judicial functions. Cases of Resident District Commissioners (RDCs) threatening to punish Magistrates for the decisions they make in their judicial capacities abound. How about the political leaders who are often heard threatening to hold demonstrations about matters pending therein? But the worst instances are the press speculations and discussions of matters pending in courts! So much for direct interferences. The indirect interferences are more grave and inhibitive. Take a case in which the tools of trade e.g. transport accommodation, books and a living wage. To deny them such tools is the the greatest of all interferences because without them, they cannot discharge their judicial functions. [37]

It is clear from the above quotation that organs that interfere with the judiciary are part of the executive arm of government. The executive arm of the state again makes the decisions concerning the payment and facilitation of the judiciary. This means that if the executive is displeased with rulings of courts on certain items, it could cut off the funds.

SAPs and the Judiciary

The most damaging aspect of the 1999 constitutional developments was the failure of the judiciary to fulfill their constitutional obligations because of donor conditionalities. As part of the IMF and World Bank cost cutting measures, government spending was severely curtailed and recruitment into the state departments frozen. The effect was that the judiciary could not render the necessary services and to fulfil its constitutional obligations. Again Justice Ntabgoba notes that:

> For several years now, the High Court has had to operate under capacity because of the so-called embargo on recruitment. It is disheartening that those who are supposed to recruit for the judiciary have always made ridiculous justifications that the embargo on recruitment includes embargo on replacement. Consequently, the judicial staff has been so depleted that it is no longer possible to operate. How can a judge, for instance, do his or her work without a secretary, without a court clerk or interpreter and without a driver? A number of Judges do not have these support staff members and yet blames for delays in trials have become a litany, not only on the lips of members of the litigating public, but also of those who have denied the judiciary the necessary employees to do the work! If I may specifically give figures with

reference to the High Court and the Magistrates' courts, the High Court which is supposed to have 30 Judges can now make do with 17 Judges. The 12 or 13 judges cannot be recruited to make the full complement, thanks to the embargo on recruitment and replacement...We are told that it is a conditionality of our donors that a recruitment and replacement embargo be clamped even on the government institutions rendering essential services like the administration of justice. Yet in the same breath we are told that it is a conditionality of the donors that the courts remove backlog in trials and that they must decongest the prisons by trying inmates on remand. Surely, either the donors or those in government charged with enabling and facilitating the Judiciary or both are not serious.[38]

This speech was made in 1996. However, a study carried out in 1999 notes that the problem still persists:

Uganda has about 350 judges and magistrates, 50 of them (14 per cent) women. This is far from what is needed. At chief magistrate level, for example, there are only 18 magistrates in service, as opposed to the established 29. At the grade one magistrate level half of the posts are vacant. The backlog of cases is thus massive. High court judges are hitherto to be found in only six upcountry stations and prison inmates on remand have had to wait for three years for this court to sit. Others have spent up to seven years in prison without being tried...[39]

In this situation, the constitutional provision that the people should have speedy hearing is undermined.[40]

Workers' rights to form/join trade unions

The judiciary is not the only area where fulfillment of constitutional provisions is diminished. There are other areas of the constitution such as the right of workers to belong to trade unions that cannot be implemented simply because of structural adjustment programmes. Article 29 (e) states that every person has a right to join associations or unions, 'including trade unions and political and other civic organisations.' And yet in some industries such as privatised hotels the employers have been preventing workers from joining or forming trade unions contrary to the constitution. In addition, the privatisation of public enterprises has undermined the capacity of workers to defend their rights through trade unions. The employees have no mechanism to enforce their rights because trade unions have been severely weakened by the very structural adjustment policies.[41] Employers have not honoured their agreements to pay adequate compensation to laid off workers. And governments, right from early independence days, have been violating some of the constitutional guarantees of workers' rights ostensibly to attract foreign investors. For example, the right to strike has always violated by governments in one way or the other.

The 1998 Land Act
Yet another matter that puts question marks on the process of constitutionalism is to do with the implementation of the 1998 Land Act, and more particularly on the issue of land tribunals. Article 243 (1) of the 1995 constitution states that parliament shall by law provide for the establishment of land tribunals. Clause (2) reads 'the jurisdiction of a land tribunal shall include –

(a)   the determination of disputes relating to the grant, lease, repossession, transfer or acquisition of land by individuals, the Uganda Land Commission or other authority with responsibility relating to land; and

(b)   the determination of disputes relating to the amount of compensation to be paid for land acquired'.

This constitutional requirement is also reflected in an elaborate form in the 1998 Land Act.[42] In fact, some provisions in section 77 of the 1998 Land Act are lifted word for word from the constitution. In the year under review the land tribunals had not been put in place. This means that not only were the constitutional provisions not implemented but also justice was denied to people because the magistrates' courts have been divested of their jurisdiction over land disputes. The people are effectively denied their constitutional right to 'a fair, speedy' hearing. The unresolved land conflicts also have an adverse effect on production especially in rural areas.

Related to this is the provision on a Land Fund intended to give loans to tenants by occupancy to acquire registrable interests and government acquisition of registered land to enable tenants gain registrable interests. An investigation into the matter revealed that the fund could not be set up because of a lack of funds and serious doubt was cast on the workability of the Land Fund even with availability of the money.[43]

The Leadership Code of Conduct
Yet another 1999 constitutional issue meriting our attention is the leadership code of conduct. Article 233 of the 1995 constitution provides for the leadership code of conduct which shall 'require specified officers to declare their incomes assets and liabilities from time to time and how they acquired or incurred them'. Article 234 provides that the Inspectorate of Government or such other authority will enforce the Leadership Code of Conduct as

parliament may by law prescribe'.[44] The implementation of this constitutional provision has been difficult. During his address to resident district commissioners, at the International Conference Centre, the Inspector of Government, Mr Jotham Tumwesigye, reported that 87 per cent of the district leaders had refused to declare their assets contrary to the constitution.

> Only 205 out of 1,659 district chairpersons and councilors had declared their assets since taking office. He also said only two out of 205 town clerks and treasurers and 605 district heads of department had declared assets.[45]

Part of the problem was that the inspectorate had not been given sufficient powers by parliament to deal with those who do not adhere to the leadership code of conduct. But the other is the conflict of interest that pervades parliament in this matter. Parliamentarians would not certainly legislate a law to catch them. The problem of conflict of interest is also pronounced in the structures of decentralisation. Many councillors are involved in procuring tenders for the supply of essential items to the districts, contrary to the principle of conflict of interest.[46]

The Human Rights Commission

Noticeable in the year under review is the work of the Uganda Human Rights Commission (UHRC). Among other things, the UHRC is mandated to investigate, on its own initiative or on a complaint made by any person or group of persons, the violation of any human right; to visit prisons, and places of detention or related facilities with a view to assessing and inspecting conditions of inmates and make recommendations; to establish a continuing programme of research, education and information to enhance respect of human rights; etc.[47] The UHRC is reported to have handled almost two thousand complaints, relating mainly to the deprivation of rights to property, violations of the right to a fair hearing, employment rights and the right to a pensions. It has also carried out educational campaigns, seminars and training programmes. Its role in contributing to the rule of law and constitutionalism was summed up by a *Monitor* editorial as follows:

> It is a sign of the complexities and possibilities in Uganda that the UHRC takes its job more seriously than many other supposedly independent human rights organisations. It has also exhibited more moral courage than some of the foreign missions which fund some of its activities, and otherwise have more leverage vis-a-vis the government than the UHRC does. For example, no Ugandan human rights organisation takes a position on such broad issues like UHRC does; speaking out on Congo, the Referendum, the right of parties to organise,

press freedom and many more...For once, here is a government funded body which is worth the tax-payers' money. The best thing those who care for human rights can do it to give the UHRC every possible support, and we hope it will live up to its expectations.[48]

Judicial Commission of Inquiry into the Police Force

The year also saw the appointment of the Judicial Commission of Inquiry into the Police Force (JCIPF).[49] The JCIPF, headed by Lady Justice Julia Sebutinde, was mandated to investigate allegations of corruption in the police force.[50] The facts revealed in the public hearings regarding the extent of corruption in the police force and abuse of human rights by police personnel shocked the nation. However, it is one thing to have a commission of inquiry and another to implement the far-reaching reforms that are recommended so that even those who are supposed to administer the law uphold the rule of law and the constitution.

Conclusion

Ninteen ninty-nine has been a year of mixed results as far as the culture of constitutionalism in Uganda is concerned. On the positive note, there were strides in the operation of the parliament especially in taming the executive that has for the greater part of the post-independence period dominated the functioning of the state machinery. We have also, and amazingly too, witnessed a state organ – the Uganda Human Rights Commission-play such a useful role in buttressing some of the fundamental freedoms and rights embedded in the constitution. In addition, the year saw the appointment of the Judicial Commission of Inquiry into the Police Force. At least this was a gesture to show that government was willing to tame some of the state organs that were meting out onto the populace the kind of state-inspired terror that characterised pre-NRM periods.

All these positive developments, however, continue to be dogged by certain drawbacks such as the overwhelming dependence of Uganda on foreign funds, the economic policies dictated by IMF and World Bank which in the final analysis undermine the otherwise useful provisions within the constitution. These include the quick subjection of individuals to a fair hearing, the right of workers to belong to a union, the establishment of tribunals crucial to the peaceful resolution of conflicts over land, etc.

The culture of constitutionalism was further dealt a blow by the continued-armed conflicts in northern and western Uganda and by the Karamojong's sporadic fighting in northeastern Uganda. This in itself could be an expression of a sense of frustration and more particularly the contradiction within the constitution which, on the one hand, provides for freedom to associate and, on the other, removes it by banning political party activities. Those who do not want to belong to the Movement seem to be denied the right to dissent or to organise.

In general, 1999 was a year in which positive developments occurred building on the very tremendous contribution by the NRM to end stat-inspired violence. However, it will be too much to expect the NRM to be a watchdog for upholding the Ugandan constitution and promoting the culture of constitutionalism. There are other things that need to be in place for this to happen such as a vibrant civil society and media. Constitutionalism has to be struggled for. Preceded by the NRA/NRM armed struggle, whatever constitutional development has been achieved so far needs to be consolidated in the coming years through mechanisms that allow peaceful dissent and assembly.

Notes

1. Interview with Joe Oloka-Onyango, Dean, Faculty of Law, Makerere University, March 10, 2000.

2. The Republic of Uganda, 1995, *Constitution of the Republic of Uganda*, Entebbe: UPPC.

3. Holger Bernt Hansen has argued that the entire process behind the 1995 constitution 'may be characterised as an unusual and pioneering approach in the history of constitution-making, a bold experiment, but it goes without saying that it is very time consuming...' Holger Bernt Hansen, 1992, 'A Long Journey Towards a New Constitution: The Ugandan Experiment in Constitution Making, Copenhagen: Centre for African Studies Working Paper No. 1992/1.

Anthony J. Regan argues that 'the NRM Government in Uganda has undertaken potentially the most far reaching constitutional reform exercise attempted in any African country in the post colonial era. Its significance is not just in the details of the innovative reform process and institutional arrangements, actual and proposed, but also in the fact of the serious attempt to make constitutionalism a reality in Uganda.' See Anthony J. Regan, 1995, 'Constitutional Reform and the Politics of the Constitution in Uganda: A Path to Constitutionalism?' in P. Langseth, J. Katorobo, E. Brett and J. Munene (eds.), *Uganda: Landmarks in Rebuilding a Nation*, Kampala: Fountain Publishers.

4. Okoth Ogendo argues 'political developments in Africa since Ghana's independence in 1957, have demonstrated again and again, however, that not only have constitutions 'failed' to regulate the exercise of power, but – which is more

devastating – they have not become as basic as the analytical traditional scholars thought they would be.' See H. W. O. Okoth-Ogendo, 1991, 'Constitutions Without Constitutionalism: Reflections on an African Political Paradox' in Issa G. Shivji (ed.), *State and Constitutionalism: An African Debate on Democracy*, Harare: SAPES Books, 199?, p.4. Even the most revered American constitution was not respected in the beginning. 'The American Constitution was drafted by 55 delegates and was officially adopted on March 4, 1789. Not all the delegates were pleased with the results. Some left before the signing ceremony. Three of those remaining refused to sign'. Batoroogwa E.K., 1995, 'New Constitution Still has Big Test,' *The New Vision* October 3: See also Clinton Rossiter, 1999, *The Federalist Papers*, New York: Mentor, 1999.

5. Mahmood Mamdani, 1991, 'Social Movements and Constitutionalism in the African Context' in Issa G. Shivji, *State and Constitutionalism: An African Debate on Democracy*, Harare: SAPES Books.

6. Prof. A. Nsibambi defines constitutionalism as the 'valuing and putting in practice democratically agreed rules of the game in deciding who gets what, how, when and for how long'. See 'Report on the International Conference on Constitutionalism in Africa: New Challenges, New Opportunities,' Kampala: Faculty of Law, February 2000.

7. See Uganda Parliamentary Debates (Hansard) second Series Vol. 63, First Session 1966-1967, Entebbe: Government Printer, p. 574.

8. The Republic of Uganda, 1967, *The Constitution of the Republic of Uganda*, Entebbe: Government Printer.

9. Nelson Kasfir, 1967, 'The 1967 Uganda Constituent Assembly Debate', *Transition*, Vol. 7, No. 33 October/November.

10. For an elaborate analysis of the relationship between the executive and the judiciary, see Joe Oloka-Onyango: 1993, 'Judicial Power and Constitutionalism in Uganda', Kampala: Center for Basic Research Working paper No. 30.

11. Oloka-Onyango, Ibid, p. 30.

12. Joseph Oloka-Onyango, 1996, 'Taming the Executive: The History of and Challenges to Uganda's Constitution-Making' in Joseph Oloka Onyango, Kivutha Kibwana and Chris Maina Peter (eds.), *Law and the Struggle for Democracy in East Africa*, Nairobi: Claripress.

13. David Watt, Rachel Flanary and Robin Theobald, 'Democratisation or the Democratisation of Corruption?

14. See J. Oloka-Onyango, 1998 'Governance, State Structures and Constitutionalism in Contemporary Uganda,' Kampala: CBR working Paper No. 52.

15. There are other reasons why neigbouring countries have been destabilising Uganda. These range from their attempt to solve their domestic problems by

presenting Uganda as a scapegoat (e.g. pre-1992 Kenya) to desire to control resources in Uganda.

16. John Kakande and Joyce Namutebi, 1999, 'Amnesty Bill Passed,' *The New Vision*, 8 December.

17. The Republic of Uganda, 1995, *Constitution of the Republic of Uganda*, Entebbe: UPPC, pp. 166-167.

18. Ibid. (The Republic of Uganda, 1995, *Constitution of the Republic of Uganda*, Entebbe: UPPC, pp. 28-29.

19. Human Rights Watch, 1999, *Hostile to Democracy: The Movement System and Political repression in Uganda*, New York: Human Rights Watch, p 85.

20. Human Rights Watch, Ibid., p 85-86.

21. Henry Ochieng, 1999, 'Parliament in Recess,' *The Monitor*, December 20.

22. Address by H.E. the president to parliament 15 September 1998 (mimeo). See also speech by Amama Mbabazi at the United Nations. 1999, 'Uganda was Dragged into the Congo Crisis,' *The New Vision* 19 April.

23. The Republic of Uganda, 1995, *The Constitution of the Republic of Uganda*, Kampala: Government of Uganda, p. 135.

24. Peter G. Mwesige, 1999, 'Parliament: A House of Scandal,' *The New Vision*, 29 December 1999.

25. Peter G. Mwesige, 1999, 'Valley Dams Report Calls For CID Probe,' *The New Vision*, 2 November.

26. Sylvia Juuko, 1999, President Sick of MPs, Bad Officials,' *The Monitor*, 27 October.

27. Sylvia Juuko, Ibid.

28. John Kakande and Felix Osike, 1999, 'MPs Hit Back at Museveni,' *The New Vision* 29, October 1999.

29. Henry Ochieng, 1999, 'Angry MPS Tell Museveni off,' *The Monitor* 29 October.

30. Peter Nyanzi, 1999, 'Delay on AES was for the Good of all,' *The New Vision*, 10 December. See also Kajabago-Ka-Rusoke, 1999, 'Museveni and the Parliament, Who is inefficient? *Sunday Vision*, 31 October.

31. Republic of Uganda, 1995, *Constitution of the Republic of Uganda*, p. 75.

32. Henry Ochieng, 1999, 'Motion to Stop MPS being Minister Sails,' *The Monitor*, 10 December.

33. J. Oloka Onyango, 1998, 'Governance, State Structures and Constitutionalism in Contemporary Uganda,' CBR Working Paper No. 52, Kampala: CBR Publications p.29.

34. 'The Referendum and Other Provisions Act, 1999', 1999, *The Uganda Gazette*, Vol. XCII No. 34.

35. The Republic of Uganda, 1995, *The Constitution of the Republic of Uganda*, Kampala: Government of Uganda, p.56.

36. *Ibid.* (ft 26) p. 83.

37. Samson James Opolot and Crispin Kintu Nyago, 2000, *Lessons of Constitutional Making in Uganda*, CBR Workshop report No. 10, Kampala: Centre for Basic Research.

38. Samson James Opolot and Crispin Kintu Nyago, Ibid., pp 38-39.

39. Henrik Hammargren, Frank Muhereza, Ase Ottosson, John Senkumba, 1999, 'Peace, democracy and Human Rights in Uganda: A String of Fragile Pearls, Stockholm: Swedish International Development Agency, p.30.

40. See article 28. The Republic of Uganda, 1995, *The Constitution of the Republic of Uganda*, p.26.

41. See Nyangabyaki Bazaara, 2000, 'Contemporary Civil Society and the Democratisation Process in Uganda: A Preliminary Exploration, Centre for Basic Research Working Paper No. 54, Kampala: Centre for Basic Research.

42. The Republic of Uganda, 1998, 'The Land Act, 1998', *The Uganda Gazette* Vol. XCI, No. 41.

43. Joyce Namutebi, 1999, 'Land Fund Can't Work,' *The New Vision* 14, September.

44. The Republic of Uganda, 1995, *Constitution of the Republic of Uganda*, pp. 144-145.

45. Anne A. Mugisa, 1999, '87% LC5s Refuse to Declare Assets,' *The New Vision* 18 November.

46. Tukahebwa notes that 'in practice LGTB [Local Government Tender Board] have tended to epitomise the financial management problems that have come along with decentralisation. Numerous press reports as well as the reports of the Auditor General, and the Inspector General of Government (IGG) have pointed out how tendering procedures were flouted resulting in inflated prices, awarding contracts to councilors themselves and even supply of "air"'. See Geoffrey B. Tukahebwa, 1998, 'The Role of District Councils in Decentralisation' in Apolo Nsibambi (ed.), *Decentralisation and Civil Society: The Quest for Good Governance*, Kampala: Fountain Publishers, p.19.

47. See articles 51 and 52 of the 1995 constitution, pp. 36-37.

48. 'Cheers for the Uganda Human Rights Commission,' *The Monitor*, 11 March 2000.

49 *The Uganda Gazette* No. 19 Vol. XCII, 23 April 1999. See also 'Judicial Commission of Inquiry into Corruption in the Police Force (Amendment) (No. 2) Notice 1999, *The Uganda Gazette* No. 59 Vol. XCII 19 November 1999.

50 Felix Osike, 1999, 'Did Karim Give Bakiza 100M/- Bribe?' *The New Vision* 23 April.

Bibliography

Address by H.E. the President to Parliament 15th September, 1998 (mimeo).

Adoko, Akena, '1967, The Constitution of the Republic of Uganda,' *Transition* Vol 7 No. 33.

Ali, Picho, 1967, 'The 1967 Republican Constitution of Uganda,' *Transition* Vol. 7, No 34.

Bazaara, Nyangabyaki, 2000, 'Contemporary Civil Society and the Democratisation Process in Uganda: A Preliminary Exploration, Centre for Basic Research Working Paper No. 54, Kampala: Centre for Basic Research.

'Cheers for the Uganda Human Rights Commission,' *The Monitor*, 11 March 2000.

Hammargen, Henrik; Muhereza, Frank; Ottosson, Ase; Senkumba, John, 1999, 'Peace, democracy and Human Rights in Uganda: A String of Fragile Pearls,' Stockholm: Swedish International Development Agency.

Hansen, Holger Bernt, 1992, 'A Long Journey Towards a New Constitution: The Ugandan Experiment in Constitution Making' Copenhagen: Centre for African Studies Working Paper No. 1992/1.

Human Rights Watch, 1999, Hostile to Democracy: The Movement System and Political repression in Uganda, New York: Human Rights Watch.

Henry Ochieng, 1999, 'Parliament in Recess,' *The Monitor*, 20 December.

'Judicial Commission of Inquiry into Corruption in the Police Force' (Amendment) (No. 2) Notice 1999, *The Uganda Gazette* No. 59 Vol. XCII November 19, 1999.

Juuko, Sylvia, 1999, 'President Sick of MPs, Bad Officials,' *The Monitor*, 27 October.

Kajabago-Ka-Rusoke, 1999, 'Museveni and the Parliament, Who is inefficient?' *Sunday Vision*, 31 October.

Kakande, John and Namutebi, Joyce, 1999, 'Amnesty Bill Passed,' *The New Vision*, 8 December.

Kakande, John and Osike, Felix, 1999, 'MPs Hit Back at Museveni,' *The New Vision*, 29 October.

Kasfir, Nelson, 1967, 'The 1967 Uganda Constituent Assembly Debate', *Transition*, Vol. 7, No. 33.

Lino Steve, 1968, 'The Uganda Constitution', *Transition* Vol. 7, No 34.

Mahmood Mamdani, 1991, 'Social Movements and Constitutionalism in the African Context' in Issa G. Shivji, *State and Constitutionalism: An African Debate on Democracy*, Harare: SAPES Books.

Mugisa, Anne A., 1999, '87% LC5s Refuse to Declare Assets,' *The New Vision*, 18 November.

Mwesige, Peter G., 1999, 'Parliament: A House of Scandal,' *The New Vision*, 29 December.

Mwesige, Peter G., 1999, 'Valley Dams Report Calls For CID Probe,' *The New Vision*, 2 November.

Namutebi, Joyce, 1999, 'Land Fund Can't Work,' *The New Vision*, 14 September.

Nyanzi, Peter, 1999, 'Delay on AES was for the Good of all,' *The New Vision*, 10 December.

Odur-Oaper, 1968, 'A Reply', *Transition* Vol. 7, No 34.

Odongo, Onyango, 1993, *Why Uganda Independence Constitution Failed*, Gulu: Lapare General Agency.

Okoth-Ogendo, H. W. O., 1999, 'Constitutions Without Constitutionalism: Reflections on an African Political Paradox' in Issa G. Shivji (ed.), *State and Constitutionalism: An African Debate on Democracy*, Harare: SAPES Books.

Oloka-Onyango, Joe 1993, 'Judicial Power and Constitutionalism in Uganda', Kampala: Center for Basic Research Working paper No. 30.

Oloka-Onyango, Joseph, 1996, 'Taming the Executive: The History of and Challenges to Uganda's Constitution-Making' in Joseph Oloka Onyango, Kivutha Kibwana and Chris Maina Peter (eds.) *Law and the Struggle for Democracy in East Africa*, Nairobi: Claripress.

Oloka-Onyango, J., 1998, 'Governance, State Structures and Constitutionalism in Contemporary Uganda,' CBR Working Paper No. 52, Kampala: CBR Publications.

Opolot, Samson James, Kintu-Nyago, Crispin, 2000, *Lessons of Constitutional Making in Uganda*, CBR Workshop report No. 10, Kampala: Centre for Basic Research.

Osike, Felix, 1999, 'Did Karim Give Bakiza 100M/- Bribe?' *The New Vision* 28, April.

Regan, Anthony J., 1995, 'Constitutional Reform and the Politics of the Constitution in Uganda: A Path to Constitutionalism?' in P. Langseth, J. Katorobo, E. Brett and J. Munene (eds.), *Uganda: Landmarks in Rebuilding a Nation*, Kampala: Fountain Publishers.

'Report on the International Conference on Constitutionalism in Africa: New Challenges, New Opportunities,' Kampala: Faculty of Law, February 2000.

Rossiter, Clinton, 1999, *The Federalist Papers*, New York: Mentor.

'The Referendum and Other Provisions Act, 1999', *The Uganda Gazette*, Vol. XCII No. 34, July 3, 1999

The Republic of Uganda, *The Constitution of the Republic of Uganda*, Kampala: Government of Uganda, 1995.

The Republic of Uganda, 1967, *The Constitution of the Republic of Uganda*, Entebbe: Government Printer.

The Republic of Uganda, 1998, 'The Land Act, 1998', *The Uganda Gazette*, Vol. XCI, No. 41.

The Uganda Gazette No. 19 Vol. XCII, April 23, 1999.

Tukahebwa, Geoffrey B., 1998, 'The Role of District Councils in Decentralisation' in Apolo Nsibambi (ed.), *Decentralisation and Civil Society: The Quest for Good Governance*, Kampala: Fountain Publishers.

Uganda Parliamentary Debates (Hansard) second Series Vol. 63, First Session 1966-1967, Entebbe: Government Printer.

'Uganda was Dragged into the Congo Crisis,' *The New Vision*, April 19, 1999.

Index

Administrations (Kingdom) bill 1966, 43

African Independence Movement (AIM), 22

African National Congress (ANC), 21

Afro-Shirazi Party (ASP), 24

All Muslim Nationalist Union of Tanzania (AMNUT), 22

Allied Democratic Forces (ADF), 47

13th amendment of 2000, 21, 29-31

Amin, 44

Amnesty bill, 47

Armed insurgence, 47-49

Balance of power, 44

Ban on political parties, 48

Bill of rights, 19, 23, 26, 46

Buganda, 41, 42

Bunyoro-Kitara, 42

Centre for Constitutional Development, 1, 2

Centre for Governance and Development, 9

Censure, 49-50

Chama Cha Mapinduzi (CCM), 24, 26

Citizen activism, 12-14

Civil organisations, 19

Civil society, 4, 7, 9, 10

Civil war, 3

Co-operative movements, 19, 20

Constituent assembly, 23, 24, 45-47

Constitution Commission, 45-47

Constitution of TANU, 24

Constitution of Uganda 1995, 40

Constitutional amendment, 9-10

Constitutional crisis 1966, 42

Constitutional review, 4, 7, 9-16

Coup d'etat, 4

Culture of constitutionalism, 2

Deportation (Validation) Act, 43

Democratic Party (DP), 41

Democracy, 21

Dictatorship, 4, 23

Egyptian musical club, 19

Emergency law, 3

Ethnic clashes, 4

Federal, 41

Foundation for African Development (FAD), 48

General elections, 3

Human rights, 45

Ibingira, Grace, 43

IMF, 55-59

Independence constitution, 19, 21

Individual merit, 46

Inter Parties Parliamentary Group, 15

Interim Constitution of,
        Uganda 1966, 42
        United Republic of Tanzania
        1965, 23-24

Judicial Commission of Inquiry into the Police Force, 59

Judicial Interpretations, 10

Judicial Service Commission, 10

Kabaka Yekka (KY), 41

Katiba Mpya-Maisha Mpya, 5

Kenya African Democratic Union (KADU), 3

Kenya African National Union (KANU), 1, 3, 4, 5, 7, 8

Kenya Peoples' Union (KPU), 3

Kenya Review Commission Act 1997, 5-6, 14

Kenya Review Commission (Amendment) Act 1998, 5, 7, 15, 16
Kenya Women Political Caucus, 6, 7
Kenyan Somalis, 3
Kenyatta, Jomo, 3
Kisanga Committee, 28-29
Kombo, Thabit, 24

Lancaster House Constitutional Conference, 3
Land Act 1998, 57
Law Society of Kenya, 12
Leadership Code of Conduct, 57-58
League of Nations, 19
Lords Resistance Army (LRA), 47
Lost counties, 41
Lukiiko, 43

Mengo government, 42
Moi, Daniel Arap, 1, 3
Monarchists, 41
Movement system, 46
Multi-party state, 21, 26, 27, 28
Multi-party system, 46
Multipartyism, 3, 4, 21
Mutesa, Edward-Kabaka of Buganda, 41
Mwinyi, Ali Hassan, 27

Nadiope, William - Kyabazinga of Busoga, 41
Nairobi City Council, 12
National Bank of Kenya, 11
National Conference, 28
National Convention Executive Council (NCEC), 1, 4, 7, 10, 14
National Convention Planning Committee (NCPC), 4
National Council of Non-Government Organisations, 6
National Rescue Action Plan, 14-15
National Resistance Movement (NRM), 45
National Social Security Fund (NSSF), 11
National Union of Tanzania Workers (NUTA), 20
Nationalist Enterprise Party (NEP), 22
Nationalists, 19
Nyalali Commission, 27-28
Nyerere, Mwalimu Julius K., 22, 23
Obote, Milton, 41, 42
Odinga, Jaramogi Oginga, 4
Odinga, Raila, 1, 8
Onapito Ekomoloit motion, 52
One-party commission, 22-23, 26
One-party state (system), 3, 21, 22, 27, 28,

Parliamentary Service Commission, 9
Party supremacy, 23, 26
People Convention Party (PCP), 22
Peoples Democratic Party (PDP), 22
Permanent Constitution of the United Republic of Tanzania 1977, 24-25
Political assassinations, 3
Political change, 41
Political stalemate, 5
Political system, 27
Presidential decree, 44
Preventive Detention Act 1992, 27
Protestant churches, 6

Referendum, 41, 42, 46
Referendum and other Provisions Act, 53
Rule of law, 45

Saba Saba, 4
Safari park, 8
Secession threats, 3
State patronage, 46
Sudan, 47
Supreme Council of Kenya Muslims, 12

Tanganyika African National Union
(TANU), 21
Tanganyika Federation of Labour
(TFL), 20
Tanganyika Law Society, 25, 26
Tanzania Peoples Defence Forces, 44
Trade unions, 19, 20

Ufungamano, 1, 5
Uganda Human Rights Commission,
58-59

Uganda Peoples Congress (UPC),
23, 41
Union of Tanganyika and Zanzibar, 22
United Tanganyika Party (UTP), 21

White paper, 21, 28-29
World Bank, 55-59
Young African Sports Club (Yanga),
19

www.ingramcontent.com/pod-product-compliance
Lightning Source LLC
Chambersburg PA
CBHW070602290326
41929CB00060B/2532